# Sustainable Marketing and the Circular Economy in Poland



*Sustainable Marketing and the Circular Economy in Poland* outlines the specific challenges around formulating an organisation's marketing strategy in line with the circular economy (CE) framework.

This book helps to solve the problem of ineffective pro-environmental programmes and marketing tools, which are currently used by enterprises to make their activities more sustainable. The authors identify key concepts and strategies of sustainable marketing to highlight the trends and development directions of marketing activities of modern enterprises. Focussing on Poland as a central case study, the book is illustrated with examples of organisations that are implementing sustainable marketing activities that are compatible with the CE model. It also presents the results of studies which examined the pro-environmental marketing efforts of small- and medium-sized enterprises, non-governmental organisations and other actors in Poland. To conclude, the authors put forward recommendations for CE network stakeholders regarding sustainable marketing management, focussing specifically on how to avoid accusations of greenwashing and other unethical organisational behaviour.

This book will be of great interest to students and scholars of green marketing, sustainable business and the CE, as well as entrepreneurs and business professionals looking to formulate sustainable marketing strategies.

**Anita Proszowska** (PhD) is an assistant professor in the Department of Business and Enterprise Management in the Faculty of Management, AGH University of Krakow. She is author of more than 90 scientific publications on marketing. She is a member of the Polish Scientific Marketing Association.

**Ewa Prymon-Ryś** (PhD) is an assistant professor in the Department of Business and Enterprise Management in the Faculty of Management, AGH University of Krakow, Poland. She is author of more than 70 scientific articles and co-author of 2 books.

**Anna Dubel** (PhD) is an assistant professor in the Department of Finance and Accounting in the Faculty of Management, AGH University of Krakow, Poland.

**Anna Kondak** (PhD) is a research assistant in the Department of Business and Enterprise Management in the Faculty of Management, AGH University of Krakow, Poland.

**Aleksandra Wilk** (PhD) is a research assistant in the Department of Business and Enterprise Management in the Faculty of Management, AGH University of Cracow, Poland.

# Routledge Focus on Environment and Sustainability

**EU Trade-Related Measures against Illegal Fishing**
Policy Diffusion and Effectiveness in Thailand and Australia
*Edited by Alin Kadfak, Kate Barclay, and Andrew M. Song*

**Food Cultures and Geographical Indications in Norway**
*Atle Wehn Hegnes*

**Sustainability and the Philosophy of Science**
*Jeffry L. Ramsey*

**Food Cooperatives in Turkey**
Building Alternative Food Networks
*Özlem Öz and Zühre Aksoy*

**The Economics of Estuary Restoration in South Africa**
*Douglas J. Crookes*

**Urban Resilience and Climate Change in the MENA Region**
*Nuha Eltinay and Charles Egbu*

**Global Forest Visualization**
From Green Marbles to Storyworlds
*Lynda Olman and Birgit Schneider*

**Sustainable Marketing and the Circular Economy in Poland**
Key Concepts and Strategies
*Anita Proszowska, Ewa Prymon-Ryś, Anna Dubel, Anna Kondak and Aleksandra Wilk*

For more information about this series, please visit: www.routledge.com/Routledge-Focus-on-Environment-and-Sustainability/book-series/RFES

# Sustainable Marketing and the Circular Economy in Poland

## Key Concepts and Strategies

**Anita Proszowska, Ewa Prymon-Ryś, Anna Dubel, Anna Kondak and Aleksandra Wilk**

Routledge
Taylor & Francis Group
LONDON AND NEW YORK

earthscan
from Routledge

First published 2024
by Routledge
4 Park Square, Milton Park, Abingdon, Oxon OX14 4RN

and by Routledge
605 Third Avenue, New York, NY 10158

*Routledge is an imprint of the Taylor & Francis Group, an informa business*



*British Library Cataloguing-in-Publication Data*
A catalogue record for this book is available from the British Library

ISBN: 978-1-032-52831-1 (hbk)
ISBN: 978-1-032-52836-6 (pbk)
ISBN: 978-1-003-40864-2 (ebk)

DOI: 10.4324/9781003408642

Typeset in Times New Roman
by KnowledgeWorks Global Ltd.

**The book was reviewed by Prof. Dr. hab. Aldona Glińska-Neweś.**

# Contents

*List of figures and tables* xi
*About authors* xii
*Acknowledgements and Financial Disclosure* xv

Introduction 1

1 The circular economy: An outline of the concept and its evolution 8

*1.1 The circular economy concept 8*
*1.2 Evolution of the circular economy concept 13*
*1.3 Key objectives and results of a circular economy 18*
*1.4 Circular economy implementation in word economies and mapping CE networks 20*
*References 24*

2 The evolution of sustainable marketing against a background of selected market changes 30

*2.1 The evolution of the conventional understanding of marketing 30*
*2.2 The beginnings of sustainable marketing and the green supply chain 32*
*2.3 Sustainability and sustainable marketing: definitions and practical examples 35*
*2.4 Adverse consumer trends slowing the development of sustainable marketing 39*
*2.5 Planned product obsolescence 42*

*2.6 Greenwashing 43*
*2.7 Trends supporting the development of sustainable attitudes 45*
*References 47*

3 The main sustainable change actors 55

*3.1 The concept of stakeholders 55*
*3.2 Groups of stakeholders in a circular economy and a sustainable change 56*
*3.3 Consumers as benefactors and the main stakeholders in sustainable change 59*
*3.4 The role of NGOs in a circular economy 60*
*3.5 The corporate sector and its involvement in sustainable change 66*
*3.6 Educators, academics and researchers promoting a circular economy 70*
*3.7 The importance of influencers and celebrity endorsement 72*
*3.8 Other sustainable stakeholders 78*
*References 85*

4 Examples of activities of enterprises in a circular economy 90

*4.1 Methods: an overview of circular economy and sustainable marketing practices 90*
*4.2 An overview of circular economy and sustainable marketing practices 91*
*4.3 Conclusions 120*
*References 122*

Conclusions 126

*Index 131*

# Figures and tables

## Figures


| | | |
|---|---|---|
| 1.1 | The circular economy concept. | 11 |
| 1.2 | How environmental regulations impact business results. | 15 |


## Tables


| | | |
|---|---|---|
| 3.1 | The roles of businesses and NGOs in implementing sustainable change | 69 |
| 3.2 | Overview of Polish, EU and European government and social programmes supporting pro-ecological market development. | 79 |

# About authors

**Anita Proszowska**, PhD, is an assistant professor in the Department of Business and Enterprise Management in the Faculty of Management, AGH University of Krakow. She is the author of more than 90 scientific publications on marketing. She is a member of the Polish Scientific Marketing Association. For over 20 years, she has analysed marketing theories and observed marketing practices and shared her knowledge with students and entrepreneurs in lectures and training sessions. She has also lectured and conducted research in Spain, Finland, Holland and Portugal. She analyses the use of marketing instruments to improve relations between different market participants, shape company images and increase the effectiveness of influencing buyers' market decisions, especially in green marketing. She has comprehensive experience in training and teaching. She has completed several international teacher training courses for higher education. She is an accredited tutoring practitioner. Her main scientific interests are customer behaviour analysis and customer experience management. Primarily, she observes differences in marketing communications depending on cultural differences between message senders and recipients. She pays particular attention to how today's consumers respond to today's biggest challenge – sustainability and especially sustainable marketing. She seeks answers on how to convince modern market participants to behave more pro-environmentally.

**Ewa Prymon-Ryś**, PhD, is an assistant professor in the Department of Business and Enterprise Management in the Faculty of Management, AGH University of Krakow. She is the author of over 70 scientific articles and co-author of two books. Her research interests include NGO marketing (she is a certified fundraiser for the Polish Fundraising Association), B2B marketing and stakeholder relationship management. She has lectured at universities in Finland and Mexico. She also conducts workshops for employees and owners of SMEs and training sessions at the postgraduate and doctoral levels. She is particularly interested in organisations (commercial and non-governmental) working for sustainable development that significantly contribute to the environment, society and the circular economy. Her current research concerns values co-created by NGOs together with their stakeholders and ways to measure stakeholder value.

**Anna Dubel**, PhD, is an assistant professor in the Department of Finance and Accounting in the Faculty of Management, AGH University of Krakow, Poland. She is an environmental economist cooperating with the European Commission, international and Polish scientific institutes and non-profit organisations in implementing scientific and applied projects related to environmental issues. She has worked for the International Institute for Applied Systems Analysis (IIASA) on the FP6 project SCENES: Water Scenarios for Europe and Neighbouring States and the FP7 project RESPONSES on effective climate change adaptation solutions in the water-agriculture-energy nexus. On her Marie Curie Fellowship, she cooperated with Fondazione ENI Enricco Mattei (FEEM) based in Venice on developing multi-criteria participatory approaches to designing economically feasible and sustainable water management and flood protection solutions. She has recently been taking part in projects related to cost-benefit analysis of low-emission transport solutions in several cities in Poland; PackAlliance: sustainable and innovative packaging; and Ecosales: ecological efficiency testing of the new directive on certain issues concerning contracts for the sale of goods, focusing on circular economy applications. She was PI of the SONATA project on Flood Risk Transfer Instruments and received a PhD grant from the Polish Ministry of Science. She participated in the Climate-KIC Pioneers into Practice programme researching the drivers of and instruments for green innovation in SMEs and start-ups in Poland and the UK at the Birmingham Science Park of Aston University. As a result, she acquired a grant from the Horizon 2020 INNOSUP-5-2014 programme and created the methodology for Towards Innovative Low Carbon SMEs affiliated with the Climate-KIC UK and co-coordinated the project. She is a CSR advisor to PARP and a Chief Expert in the Environmental Protection Institute IOŚ-PIB. She is the author or co-author of more than 70 peer-reviewed publications.

**Anna Kondak**, PhD, is a research assistant in the Department of Business and Enterprise Management in the Faculty of Management, AGH University of Krakow. She specialises in marketing, especially modern forms of marketing communication via social media. Her current research interests mainly concern trends in contemporary marketing concepts and activities, including sustainable marketing in a circular economy, sensory marketing and neuromarketing. She is co-author of a publication on contemporary consumers sharing transport services. She is involved in project work covering innovative tools and techniques stimulating the green behaviour of young adults, the attitudes and preferences of various stakeholders on ways of sorting and utilising waste, and implementing innovative devices for selective waste collection.

**Aleksandra Wilk**, PhD, is a researcher and teaching assistant in the Department of Business and Enterprise Management in the Faculty of Management, AGH University of Cracow. Her research interests include corporate social responsibility, sustainable marketing and organisational and civic behaviour. She is a member of the 'Green Team Research' group that studies pro-ecological behaviour by young adults. A large part of this project is devoted to aspects of the circular economy, waste segregation and re-management practices, and making young adults aware of the significant role of their pro-environmental habits. She is the author of publications on CSR influences on organisational practices and analyses of the image of socially responsible companies. She has also investigated motives for undertaking civic organisational behaviour.

# Acknowledgements and Financial Disclosure

The publication was financially supported by the AGH University of Krakow, Project Excellence Initiative – Research University in AGH.

# Introduction

Sustainability is about ensuring that future generations have at least as good living conditions as us. Over the years, the development of civilisation has been guaranteed by human intelligence and man's drive to create new inventions. As a species, humans are incredibly creative and able to innovate, adapt to many circumstances and collaborate on an astonishing scale. This should ensure continual improvement in the living conditions and security of humanity. However, according to a team of Swedish researchers led by Peter S. Jørgensen (2023), the human species has been too successful and in some ways has become too intelligent to ensure its future prosperity. In the course of their evolution, organisms develop certain traits and defence mechanisms that allow them to survive on the planet. However, due to environmental changes, these traits may cease to play their role or prove harmful over time. Too much creativity in some areas results in neglect in others. Today, global companies, often richer than some countries, are a source of innovation aiming for sustainability and development rather than widespread social welfare. They seek to maximise profits by satisfying the selected needs of a part of society, forgetting about the impact of their practices on the rest of the world. In this way, the innovations generated are a source of danger to civilisation and lead to the appearance of so-called evolutionary traps. Researchers have distinguished 14 such traps including climate change, environmental pollution, misguided artificial intelligence and the spread of infectious diseases (Jørgensen et al., 2023). According to these authors, in today's global systems, social and environmental problems arise in places far removed from the societies that could have prevented them. Dealing with them often requires international cooperation, which is at odds with the interests of individual corporations or impact groups. Under these conditions, sustainability, as an action to ensure that future generations have at least the living conditions in which we live, seems a challenge beyond society's capacity. Realising this should convince us that we need to foster a capacity for collective human action and create an environment where it can thrive.

In public discourse, international institutions and pro-environmental organisations convince today's societies of a need for radical changes in

DOI: 10.4324/9781003408642-1

lifestyles not only to prevent the lowering of the standard of living of future generations but also primarily to prevent a future global climate catastrophe. It is becoming increasingly clear that general ideas of sustainable development as a basis for building management strategies are not enough. A more radical concept, a practical implementation of the sustainable development goals, is the circular economy.

According to the definition adopted by the European Union (EU), the circular economy is about maintaining the value of products, raw materials and resources for as long as possible by putting them back in their life cycle at the end of their use to minimise the generation of waste. To optimise these processes, concerted action by all market participants and coordination by governments and international institutions is necessary. Simply making citizens aware of optimising these processes is not enough. They must be given support and tools to do so effectively.

It is also necessary to have the knowledge, tools, instruments, procedures and, of course, financial resources to implement these programmes. However, the most important factor in the success of implementation of a circular economy is people and their belief in the purposefulness of these programmes. This guarantees the involvement of consumers and other market participants in the implementation of a circular economy. It should be borne in mind that a circular economy is based on rigid rules of rationalisation of resource management, which involves restrictions and a reduction in the quality of life of the people and businesses implementing it. This is more difficult for lower-income and technologically backward societies to accept. That is why the introduction of circular economy regulations has met less acceptance in Poland than, for example, in other European Union countries. In Poland, an additional factor slowing down the introduction of a circular economy is a geographically based attachment to fossil fuels (and coal in particular) as energy sources.

According to a recent report by The World Bank (Akbar et al., 2023), Poland has made clear progress over the past 30 years regarding resource efficiency and environmental protection. However, compared to other EU countries, its performance is not very satisfactory. For example, Poland generates 150 kg of waste per 1,000 euros of gross domestic product (GDP), while the EU average, excluding mineral waste, is 65 kg. Despite these as yet unsatisfactory results, our country is making evident efforts to become more circular, with a strategic roadmap for a closed-circle economy adopted by the government in 2019 providing direction. The map is followed by detailed regulations and financial resources to support a circular transformation, which are available, among others, from European Funds and National Fund for Environmental Protection and Water Management (NFOŚiGW) resources. The main barriers to development of a circular economy have been identified as follows:

- Low environmental awareness on the part of market participants. Sustainable economic processes require highly qualified personnel, frequently

with new skills and comprehensive expertise. A lack of personnel prepared to implement such processes results in competence gaps often being experienced by market participants.
- Financial, organisational, technical and technological resource investment in a circular economy takes a relatively long time to pay off. Similarly, identifying and implementing new applications for existing solutions (adaptation) and generating new solutions (innovation) present a challenge.

These problems will not be solved at the level of individuals or individual companies. More intensive efforts are needed at the national and global levels. The World Bank Report suggests a more intensive emphasis on the benefits of implementing circular economy principles and educational activities and supporting circular economy business models. Intensifying cooperation between science and business to develop further solutions is considered most helpful in accelerating the transformation. It will be necessary to support and promote the circular economy through research, studies, reports, public discussions and consultations on all practices related to a sustainable transformation. The present publication fits these expectations very well.

Each element in the modern global system influences the others and can shape the surrounding reality. One tool that is often used for this purpose is marketing. Marketing has accompanied humanity since the emergence of social life and has helped influence the attitudes and behaviour of market participants from the beginning. It is no secret that many entrepreneurs use it to increase the number of buyers of their products. Over the years, thanks to developments in technology and knowledge of human behaviour, techniques for influencing message audiences have become increasingly influential. This has the effect of making it more popular to buy new and less necessary products. As a result of too much competition, there is a massive overproduction of goods in virtually every area of human life. And the more products on the market, the more buyers are persuaded to buy new things that they need less and less.

For years, there has been talk in the public sphere about a need to change the lifestyles of modern societies. Scientists present research results showing how damaging human activity is to the climate and what needs to be done to stop environmental degradation. We are becoming increasingly aware of what lies behind very cheap food, clothes and shoes. We know how much it costs to have fruit and vegetables available worldwide that only grow in selected places on Earth. We could go on for a long time listing market phenomena and human behaviour the negative impact of which on human well-being has long been proven. However, looking at the behaviour of many of today's consumers, it may seem that this information has not reached them. The situation is no better on the part of the providers of goods. Their ever-increasing marketing activity aims to convince market participants to buy more products they do not need. The aim is to maximise sales regardless of the cost to the environment.

Even though today there is a gradually growing group of customers aware of the existing risks, they cannot independently verify information about offers and make rational choices. A sensible choice should be understood as one that considers sustainability principles. Today's product offerings are more technologically advanced, and assessing the environmental impact of their use and disposal is more complicated. The customer, who usually does not have specialised knowledge, must rely on information from the manufacturer, which often does not include the environmental impact of an offer.

Nowadays, the appearance of a given market offering results from the technological process that led to its creation and the use of specific material, financial and human resources. In each area, elements with a negative environmental impact may appear. These may include the following:

- pollutants emitted during production;
- post-production waste;
- misallocation of natural resources (exceptionally scarce mineral resources);
- deterioration of human and animal welfare during and after production (occupational diseases of humans and over-exploitation of animal health and strength).

In addition to all this, there is also an opportunity cost: instead of producing things people do not need and convincing them to buy them, one can make more necessary products or do nothing and relax.

Theoretically, the idea of sustainability and green marketing is appealing to audiences. However, implementing it involves a radical change in habits and, at least in the initial stage, an increase in the cost of living (consumers) and operating (companies). On the one hand, to convince individual consumers to live more sustainably one must convincingly explain why they should change. On the other hand, businesses will only commit to sustainability if they are confident that this is what consumers expect. With the popularisation of sustainable marketing solutions, among other things the consumer:

- will not be afraid of fewer more expensive offerings on the market because she/he will know that she/he is buying something of greater value that will stay with her/him for longer and better meet her/his needs;
- will accept higher energy prices because she/he will be sure that they guarantee her/him cleaner air and a healthier life;
- will be more willing to engage in sustainable development activities because she/he will be deeply convinced of their necessity;
- will accept some inconveniences associated with a circular economy because she/he will appreciate its economic and climate benefits.

Traditional marketing supports traditional linear economy models. In these models, satisfying consumer needs is most often understood as acquiring more products. Changes are needed in how consumers define their needs and how providers of goods and services can meet them in a more sustainable manner.

Today's market participants must determine how to change their attitudes and behaviour to more sustainable ones.

For sustainable development and the spread of the circular economy, the most crucial factor is human beings and their conviction of the inevitability of these changes. This publication aims to systematise knowledge about green orientations in individual areas of human life and to identify arguments and motivation systems that can convince people to implement them. The authors seek answers to make people more engaged in a circular economy and satisfied customers. Both are possible at the same time. The definition of marketing will not change. Marketing is still (and will be) delivery of customer satisfaction at a profit. Only the source of satisfaction is changing. In the case of Poland, a circular economy is a very long-term goal. Poland's economic and mental backwardness mean that it is only at the beginning of the road to achieving this goal. A beginning that can be defined by the pursuit of sustainable development, ultimately leading to a circular economy. This publication includes a presentation of examples of practices that Polish companies define as elements of a circular economy. When carefully analysing them, one may have doubts whether they can really be included in this group of practices. On more detailed analysis, it may turn out that they are manifestations of greenwashing rather than a circular economy or sustainable development.

After analysing the strategies of some market giants, one may question whether marketing can be sustainable. However, being aware of the current climate situation, one has to conclude that it simply has to be. A way must be found for consumers to like:

- longevity (i.e. encouraging extended use or resisting obsolescence);
- leasing (i.e. personal social services or servitisation, slowing the loop by providing access rather than ownership);
- reuse (i.e. extended use or postponing obsolescence by extending product life);
- recycling (i.e. recovery or reversing obsolescence by extending material life).

The subjects of the analysis are individuals, their attitudes and the determinants of pro-environmental behaviour. Extracting this information will allow messages to be shaped to help convince people of specific sustainable behaviours and implement programmes based on them. A suitably motivated market participant will adopt existing sustainable solutions and look for the next ones.

This monograph is divided in four chapters to achieve its objective.

- Chapter 1. The Circular Economy – An Outline of the Concept and Its Evolution (the concept, its evolution, what it is, related concepts, CE networks). This provides a general characterisation of a circular economy, describes its development and clarifies its definition.

- Chapter 2. The Evolution of Sustainable Marketing Against a Background of Selected Market Changes. This includes a description of changes in the philosophy and understanding of the role of marketing from being a tool to stimulate and direct demand to ecological and social marketing to sustainable marketing. It also includes information on the megatrends in consumption most relevant to the development of sustainable marketing. An overview of unfavourable consumer trends slowing the development of sustainable marketing and a discussion of the greenwashing phenomenon are also provided.
- Chapter 3. The Main Sustainable Change Actors. This identifies the key stakeholders in sustainable consumption and describes their roles in implementing the sustainability concept. It also identifies the drivers of their engagement.
- Chapter 4. Examples of Activities of Enterprises in a Circular Economy. Practices related to the circular economy originating among enterprises operating in Poland are presented and discussed. The chapter also includes an overview of Polish, EU and European government programmes and social initiatives that promote pro-ecological innovations, sustainable technologies and ecological business practices that can support the implementation of sustainable marketing practices and the circular economy.
- Conclusions. This presents prospects for sustainable marketing, its future challenges and development directions, in which the presumed future principles of sustainable marketing are presented. Based on previous summaries of the state of knowledge and assessment of the current market situation, the leading marketing paradigms as tools supporting the development of a circular economy are identified. Special attention is paid to the younger generation, whose attitudes today will be essential for future market decisions in entire societies.

This monograph may constitute a textbook at the level of higher education (undergraduate or graduate) and vocational and post-secondary schools with an educational profile that is thematically similar to a circular economy and sustainable marketing. It is dedicated to scientists, people from academia and teachers, business practitioners and people involved in the above-mentioned thematic areas.

This monograph responds to the growing interest in circular economy in Poland and worldwide. It characterises the concept and the consequences of its implementation. It describes the course of marketing evolution to the sustainable marketing formula and defines it as a key tool for introducing the principles of circular economy. At the same time, it emphasises the high level of difficulties in implementing solutions developed in developed countries in Poland.

## References

Akbar, S., Behrens, A., Philipp, F., & Liverani, A. (2023). Diagnostic Analysis for Circular Economy Interventions in Poland. https://documents.worldbank.org/pt/publication/documents-reports/documentdetail/099110623093517982/p1745960111a6e0000bdf80d1e97c5abe4b

Jørgensen, P. S., Weinberger, V. P., & Waring, T. M. (2023). Evolution and sustainability: gathering the strands for an Anthropocene synthesis. *Philosophical Transactions of the Royal Society B*, *379*(1893), 20220251. https://doi.org/10.1098/rstb.2022.0251

# 1 The circular economy

## An outline of the concept and its evolution

### 1.1 The circular economy concept

The emergence of the circular economy (CE) concept resulted from a long-term search for solutions to emerging environmental issues which research put on the worldwide political agenda. In 1987, the Brundtland Commission published a report entitled 'Our Common Future' which defined sustainable development as 'development that meets the needs of the present without compromising the ability of future generations to meet their own needs' (UN, 1987, p. 43). Since the 1970s, many models have been employed to provide scientific guidance on strategic and policy developments, starting with Club of Rome publications based on World3 model simulations of such variables as population, food production, industrialisation, pollution and consumption of non-renewable natural resources, showing their exponential growth, while the ability of technology to increase resources only grows linearly (Meadows et al., 1972). These revelations led to exploration of possibilities of altering the modelled growth trends of the five variables in various scenarios. The findings of subsequent modelling (Meadows et al., 1992) show that although we are closer to 'overshoot and collapse', sustainability is still an achievable goal.

Since then, as a result of deterministic experimental research, strategic and political commitments have been mobilised in order to effectively implement a sustainable agenda. Responding to physical climatic and environmental trends, recent environmental policies include the European Green Deal, sectoral directives and strategies (e.g., the Water Framework Directive and related 'daughter directives'), the European Union (EU) Climate Adaptation Strategy, the EU Circular Economy Action Plan (CEAP), CE-related directives (EC, 2017, 2018a, 2018b, 2018c, 2018d, and 2019,), Intergovernmental Panel on Climate Change practices and publications, the Paris Agreement, Conference of Parties meetings and various platforms (e.g., the Mission Ocean, Seas and Waters Implementation Support Platform, the European Climate- Adaptation platform, A Soil Deal for Europe Mission Implementation Platform, the Ocean and Water Knowledge System Implementation Platform and the EU Soil Observatory platform). Moreover, in order to facilitate

DOI: 10.4324/9781003408642-2

the implementation of climate and environmental policies, a considerable amount of funding has been mobilised, including EU funds for research and in particular Horizon Europe funding.

In a sustainable development paradigm an important challenge is to transform economies from the commonly prevailing linear model to a circular model. The main aim of this change is to keep resources which have been extracted and utilised in the loop as long as possible and minimise waste generation. Therefore, durability of product use and biodegradability of product elements are important features. The change is implemented in various phases of product development from cradle to grave, including design, production, use and disposal. In economics, the development of circular systems is possible in a holistic (pan-sectoral) approach to value and supply chains. The basis for this type of practice is processes designed with industrial symbiosis models, extended helix models or circular clusters (Gue et al., 2020; Pamučar et al., 2023; Przygodzki, 2022). Social engagement is a pre-condition for transformation towards a CE. This engagement entails extended responsibility of producers on the supply side of goods and service markets, including supply-chain management (Carter & Rogers, 2008), and of consumers on the demand side, including environmentally conscious product selection, responsible brand selection, prosumption behaviour and a restrictive approach to consumption.

The theoretical conception of a CE grew out of the concepts of sustainable development, sustainability, green growth (Organisation for Economic Co-operation and Development (OECD), 2017), a green economy (European Environment Agency (EEA), 2019), decoupling (Sanyé-Mengual et al., 2019) and degrowth (Kallis, 2017; Khmara & Kronenberg, 2018).

The concepts of sustainability and sustainable development have dominated the international development policy arena. In particular, policies have recently focused on addressing climate change (Aven, 2020), reducing fossil fuel emissions (Leal Filho et al., 2019), the transition to renewable energy (Wackernagel et al., 2017) and the transition to a CE (Ozili, 2021). At the same time, research has striven to identify factors that promote or hinder the attainment of sustainable development goals, including long-lasting socio-economic benefits for all people and the environment, in order to better inform policy decisions related to the implementation of the United Nations Sustainable Development Goals in many countries worldwide (Ozili, 2022). The sustainable development and the sustainability concepts also inspired further ideas. Green growth (OECD, 2017) concept is similar to the sustainable development idea, but with a focus on fostering economic growth and development, while ensuring that natural assets continue to provide the resources and environmental services on which the human well-being relies. Adding to that, the green economy strives to transform the dominant approach to economy, which encourages waste and triggers resource scarcity, into a low-carbon, resource-efficient and socially inclusive economic model. The decoupling concept focuses on the decoupling of economic growth, in terms of gross domestic product, from the environmental impact and resource use. As indicated by Sanyé-Mengual et al. (2019), decoupling takes place 'when resource use or some environmental pressure either grows at a slower rate than the economic activity that is causing it (relative decoupling) or declines while the economic activity continues to grow (absolute decoupling)' (IRP et al., 2017). At the same time, the degrowth idea is overall critical to the concept of growth in gross domestic product as a measure of economic development (Hickel, 2021; Kallis et al., 2018; Trainer, 2012).

Rapid population and urbanisation growth are increasing the generation of solid waste and demand for natural resources. In both scientific and practical contexts, many sustainable development models and frameworks have been developed (e.g., Duraiappah et al., 2014; Purvis et al., 2020). However, a three-pillar sustainability framework is a widely accepted and applied solution-oriented approach (Clune & Zehnder, 2020). The three pillars are environmental dimension, economic dimension and social dimension. The environmental dimension of sustainable development consists of physical integrity, biological diversity, resource efficiency and environmental purity achieved with technology and innovation. The economic dimension of sustainable development consists of economic viability, local prosperity, employment quality and social equity achieved with economic and financial incentives. The social dimension of sustainable development consists of community well-being, local development and cultural richness achieved by means of law and governance. Recent studies have suggested other dimensions of sustainable development, such as governance (Stojanović et al., 2016); technological or technical, including life-cycle sustainability assessment (Finkbeiner et al., 2010); cultural (Brocchi, 2010); and knowledge (Mebratu, 2001; Ozili, 2022).

A review of the evolution of sustainability models over the past few decades (Clune & Zehnder, 2020) shows that the three-pillar framework can effectively help translate complex sustainability issues into ideas that are better understood and applicable by communities and economic stakeholders. In addition, full transparency of aims and practices creates a necessary and often sufficient foundation for successful, scalable, more rapidly deployable and culturally acceptable sustainability solutions. Moreover, numerous case studies show that sustainability solutions which involve good governance, implementation of technology and creation of market incentives are most effective and durable (Clune & Zehnder, 2020).

Based on an extensive study of the concepts of sustainability and the CE, Geissdoerfer et al. (2017) define sustainability as 'the balanced integration of economic performance, social inclusiveness, and environmental resilience, to the benefit of current and future generations'. They also define a CE as 'a regenerative system in which resource input and waste, emission and energy leakage are minimised by slowing, closing and narrowing material and energy loops. This can be achieved through long-lasting design, maintenance, repair, reuse, remanufacturing, refurbishing and recycling' (Geissdoerfer et al., 2017).

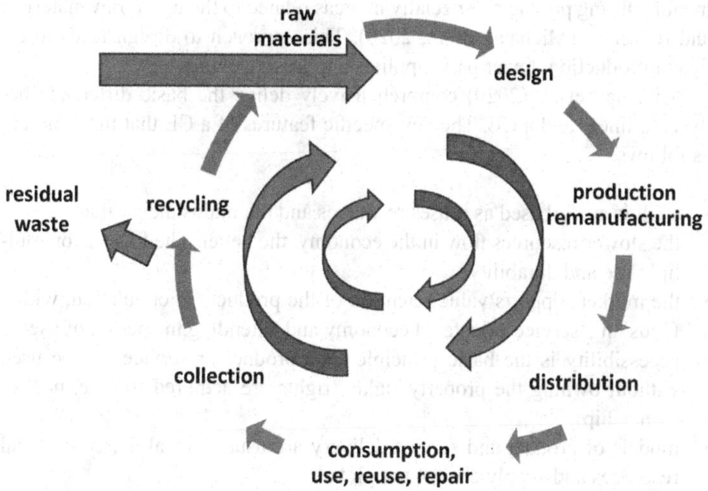


*Figure 1.1* The circular economy concept.

*Source*: Author.

A linear economy is characterised by a one-way flow of materials. Raw materials are transformed into products to later become waste. Disposal of waste is the end of a product's life, whereas in CE models waste collection adds to the stock of raw materials through recycling. Moreover, product design supports more sustainable material use, and remanufacturing, reuse, repair and zero-emission or low-emission transport used in the distribution of the products contribute to a more positive environmental effect.

As Figure 1.1 shows, the essence of a CE is striving to keep resources in circulation for as long as possible by means of various practices undertaken during the product life cycle (e.g., eco-design, remanufacturing, reuse, repairing and recycling), leading to minimisation of the amount of waste generated.

Life cycle analysis supports the design of products and services by identifying in the various phases of their life cycles environmental impacts such as water-related impacts (quality and quantity); soil pollution and degradation; air contamination (emissions, e.g., $NO_x$, $SO_x$, $PM_{10}$ and $PM_{2.5}$); climate-related impacts (measured with $CO_2$ emissions); noise emissions; energy consumption by source (e.g., lignite, brown coal, gas, nuclear, renewable energy sources; photovoltaics, wind, geothermal, water, etc.); natural resource depletion; landscape impacts; natural ecosystems and biodiversity degradation.

Another supporting method, especially in the design process, is designed for the environment, which involves changing the processes of designing and manufacturing products, especially in areas related to the use of raw materials and recycling (Michalak et al., 2020). This approach to design leads to efficient production, fewer part suppliers and less inventory.

Michalak et al. (2020) comprehensively define the basic difference between a linear and a CE. The key specific features of a CE that they find are as follows:

- a CE is stock-based as it uses resources and maintains their value;
- the slower resources flow in the economy, the better. The focus is on multiple use and durability;
- the market supports value retention of the products in circulation, with a focus on a service-orientated economy and extending the period of use;
- accessibility is the basic principle. The product or service can be used without owning the property rights (rights are acquired for use, not for ownership);
- models of product and service delivery are usually local, based on local resources and supply chains, not global;
- a focus on material and resource sufficiency and efficiency;
- a focus on extending service life, sharing and increasing attractiveness (upgrading);
- design is becoming the most important process. It covers the entire product life cycle, including the possibility of repair and modernisation (e.g., modular design and eco-design);
- prosumers are becoming active market actors, being at the same time producers and consumers of a given good, for example, energy.

According to the Ellen MacArthur Foundation (2012), the basic principles of a CE are as follows:

- designing out waste;
- building resilience through diversity;
- relying on energy from renewable sources;
- thinking in terms of systems.

According to Michalak et Al. (2020), the principles related to loops in a CE are as follows:

- the smaller the loop, the more profitable and resource-efficient the practice;
- loops have no beginning and no end;
- the speed of resource flow in circulation is important – the slower the circulation, the better;
- continuation of ownership is profitable – reuse, repair and regeneration without changing ownership protect against double transaction costs.

In conclusion, it is worth noting that a CE operationalises the concept of sustainable development and the Sustainable Development Goals (SDGs). In particular, a CE is dedicated to implementing the following goals: SDG9 – Industry, Innovation and Infrastructure, and SDG12 – Responsible Consumption and Production. SDG9 is focused on sustainable industrialisation, increased efficiency of resource use and greater adoption of clean and environmentally sound technologies and industrial processes (UN, 2015). SDG12 sets targets to achieve, by 2020, environmentally sound management of chemicals and all waste throughout its life cycle and, by 2030, sustainable management and efficient use of natural resources; to reduce food losses along production and supply chains; to substantially reduce waste generation through prevention, reduction, recycling and reuse and to encourage companies, especially large and transnational companies; to adopt sustainable practices and to integrate sustainability information in their reporting cycle (UN, 2015). This leads to the development of ESG reporting. Therefore, it can be concluded that a CE strives to develop and implement new technologies, to combine business models with eco-innovation in order to increase productivity and minimise waste, whereas sustainable development sets the conceptual frames and the direction of sustainable change.

## 1.2 Evolution of the circular economy concept

The CE concept has deep-rooted origins in the following schools of thought: regenerative design (Lyle, 1994), performance economy (Stahel, 2010), cradle to cradle (McDonough & Braungart, 2010), industrial ecology (Graedel and Allenby, 1995), blue economy (Pauli, 2010), biomimicry (Benyus, 2002) and permaculture (Ellen MacArthur Foundation, 2012; Mollison & Holmgren, 1978).

In the 1960s, depletion of natural resources and overpopulation started to be concerns on the science-policy agenda. This led to the emergence of sustainable development, corporate social responsibility (CSR), CE and related concepts.

Ayres and Kneese (1969) introduced analysis of material balances, including analysis of energy flows (Considine & Larson, 2006). In 'The Economy as Circular Flow', Leontief (1991) developed the theory of input-output analysis, which helps in designing a CE as it quantifies the interdependencies between various industry sectors in an economy, which are expressed as flows from one sector to another measured in monetary or mixed units. Pearce et al. (1989) defined the 'green economy' concept in 'Blueprint for a Green Economy'. Next, McDonough and Braungart (2010) in 'Cradle to Cradle: Remaking the Way We Make Things' called for a switch from cradle-to-grave thinking to cradle-to-cradle thinking, which closes the loop, creates circularity and extends the life of a product or service. Recently, the industrial symbiosis approach has researched and designed relations between industrial entities and their processes so that waste from one process becomes raw material for another (Gue et al., 2020).

An important concept for the implementation of a CE, CSR, can be traced back to the 1960s and it has evolved since then, substantially supporting the transition from a linear to a CE by driving changes in companies. The European Commission (EC, 2011) has recommended that to fully exercise their CSR, enterprises should have in place a process to integrate social, environmental, ethical and human rights concerns in their business operations and core strategy in cooperation with stakeholders. CSR is defined in ISO 26000 as an international standard developed to help organisations effectively assess and address social responsibilities that are significant and relevant to their:

- mission and vision,
- operations and processes,
- customers, employees, communities and other stakeholders
- and environmental impact (TEEB, 2010).

The evolution of CSR can be observed from the conventional CSR approach in which responsible practices are driven by a desire to share business success with the wider societal environment (public relation focus) to the contemporary CSR approach in which social value creation is aligned with the core purpose of the business to generate profit. This has led to the societal entrepreneurship approach (Mair & Marti, 2006), which involves innovative use and combination of resources to pursue opportunities to catalyse social change and/or address social needs. Contemporary CSR can also be implemented based on recognition of social or environmental innovation, in which businesses or projects treat specific social or environmental needs as business opportunities. In such cases, business ideas and models are created on a foundation of social or environmental innovation. This approach is highlighted in the environmental context by Porter and van der Linde (1995), who state that properly designed environmental standards can trigger innovations that lower the total cost of a product or improve its value. Such innovations allow companies to use a range of inputs – from raw materials to energy to labour – more productively, thus offsetting the costs of improving environmental impacts and ending stalemate. Ultimately, this enhanced resource productivity makes companies more competitive, not less. Successful environmentalists, regulatory agencies and companies will reject old trade-offs and build on the underlying economic logic that links the environment, resource productivity, innovation and competitiveness (Porter & van der Linde, 1995). This approach is presented in Figure 1.2.

CSR is operationalised by the Global Reporting Initiative (GRI) standards, which create a universal framework and set of disclosures to meet all sustainability reporting needs, from comprehensive reports to issue-specific

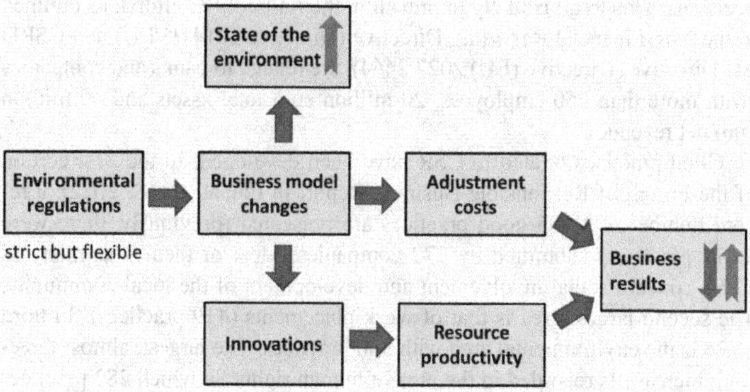


*Figure 1.2* How environmental regulations impact business results.

*Source*: Author.

disclosures. Since 2000, the GRI sustainability reporting standards have been used by thousands of organisations in more than 90 countries to publicly report impacts on the economy, the environment and society.

Other environmental certification standards are, for example, EMAS ISO 14001 and the Eco-design Management ISO 14006 standards. In addition, other approaches to incentivise and implement sustainability in the business sector have been developed, such as the triple bottom line and environmental social governance (ESG).

The triple bottom line concept underlines the fact that companies should commit to measuring their social and environmental impacts. It consists of three Ps: profit, people and the planet. As is discussed at Harvard Business School online (accessed 15.09.2023), firms can use these categories to conceptualise their environmental responsibility and determine any negative social impacts to which they might be contributing. Based on this analysis companies can introduce sustainable practices in their business operations, including their supply chains, choosing conscientiously responsible business partners and utilising renewable energy sources, among other things, in order to positively impact society and the environment, in addition to turning a profit. Moreover, in an environmentally conscientious society with growing environmental awareness, embracing sustainable business strategies can be highly attractive to investors. The triple bottom line approach was designed mainly for internal management practices, whereas ESG metrics are considered a third-party measurement of those procedures, 'holding businesses publicly accountable to focus on more sustainable practices in addition to financial profit' (Harvard Business School online, accessed 15.09.2023). Therefore, environmentally conscious investors also consult ESG metrics when making investment decisions. This trend is likely to prevail in the future. ESG efforts, as outlined in the Non-Financial Reporting Directive (Directive 2014/95/EU) and CSRD EU Directive (Directive (EU) 2022/2464), are related to banks and companies (with more than 250 employees, 20 million euro total assets and 40 million euro net revenue).

Good practices related to CSR have been developed. In the 21st edition of the Forum of Responsible Business Report in Poland (FOB, 2022), a record number of 1,705 good practices are presented (previously, there were 1,677 practices) submitted by 272 companies. Most of them – as many as 477 – concern social involvement and development of the local community. The second largest area is that of work placements (419 practices). In third place is the environmental area with 360 practices. The largest, almost threefold, increase Is recorded in the area of human rights, in which 282 practices are presented. Traditionally, the category concerning organisational governance is less numerous (75 practices). Good CE practices can be found at:

- The European Circular Economy Stakeholder Platform (https://circulareconomy.europa.eu/platform/en/good-practices, accessed 15.09.2023).
- BusinessEurope showcases examples of EU companies' efforts on the Circulary platform (http://www.circulary.eu/, accessed 15.10.2023).
- Circular Economy Overview 2021 (Circular Economy Overview 2021 (eib.org), accessed 10.10.2023).
- Synergic Circular Economy across European Regions – SCREEN Laboratory, which has defined replicable eco-innovative and horizontal business models in different value chains (SCREEN Laboratory (screen-lab.eu), accessed 15.10.2023).
- Fostering Industrial Symbiosis for a Sustainable Resource Intensive Industry across the extended Construction Value Chain (FISSAC project - a new Industrial Symbiosis model for the Construction industry | European Circular Economy Stakeholder Platform (europa.eu), accessed 21.10.2023).
- Resource Efficient Business Models (REBus, accessed 20.10.2023).
- Food and Drink Europe, CEAP (FoodDrinkEurope position: CEAP – FoodDrinkEurope: FoodDrinkEurope/, accessed 20.12.2019). See also Michalak et al. (2020).

In order to help investors and companies to make informed decisions on environmentally sustainable practices and investments, to determine the degree of sustainability, to facilitate the transition of polluting sectors and to foster transparency of sustainability efforts of companies, the EU Taxonomy was developed. The EU Taxonomy (EU Taxonomy Navigator (europa.eu), accessed 10.09.2023) is a system for classifying economic activities in terms of their compliance with the environmental objectives of the EU, and it is part of the EU strategy to increase sustainable investment and realise the European Green Deal. It has the following six climate and environmental objectives:

- climate change mitigation;
- climate change adaptation;
- sustainable use and protection of water and marine ecosystems;
- transition to a CE;
- pollution and prevention control,
- protection and restoration of biodiversity and ecosystems.

As can be seen, a transition to a CE is one of the important aims. In addition, the EU is mainstreaming the 'First Do No Harm' principle and screening EU member state proposals applying for EU funding for impacts on climate. This should help to only implement practices that will have positive or neutral impacts on the environment or climate change.

In order to operationalise implementation of the sustainable development concept, there are other incentives in the application process for Next Generation EU Funds. In particular, every proposal should comply with the sustainable development principle and among other things with the CE, including waste and recycling. Therefore, the proposal should have no negative impact on waste generation and recycling. This can be achieved, for example, by selecting optimal technical solutions in terms of the use of materials and natural resources in the project. Durability of products should be ensured, and repairing should be planned in the event of a failure. Waste generated during the implementation of the project that cannot be reused should be disposed of in accordance with applicable regulations. In addition, there should be no long-term storage of environmentally hazardous waste.

In a recent update of the paper 'Conceptualising the Circular Economy', Kirchherr et al. (2023) analysed 221 recent CE definitions and noticed the following:

- the concept has undergone both consolidation and differentiation in the past five years;
- the concept definitions have been developed more in academically relevant than practical terms;
- increasingly fundamental systemic shifts are recommended to enable a CE, particularly in supply chains;
- sustainable development is frequently considered the principal aim of a CE, but it is not evident if a CE can support both environmental sustainability and economic development;
- recent studies argue that a CE transition relies on a broad alliance of stakeholders, including producers, consumers, policymakers and scholars.

Schöggl et al. (2020) reviewed 3,822 journal papers on CE published between 2000 and 2019 and concluded that CE research has grown exponentially but its thematic diversity has only slowly increased and that waste and recycling research and economic and environmental focuses dominate in the scientific literature. Moreover, Schöggl et al.'s (2020) longitudinal study of CE literature revealed a growing dichotomy between the fields of optimisation, waste and efficiency-related work, on the one hand, and those of innovation and business model-related work, on the other hand. This study also indicated that while sustainability research addresses economic and environmental issues, social topics remain underrepresented or are even neglected.

## 1.3 Key objectives and results of a circular economy

The overarching aim of transforming an economy from a linear approach to a circular one is to reduce negative environmental impacts and boost inclusive green growth. This results in resource savings (including materials, water and energy) and a reduction of emissions and waste levels. The expected positive impacts also include local economic development due to shortened supply chains and focusing on local suppliers. Moreover, indirect impacts can also be recognised such as spillover effects and wider adoption of environmentally friendly practices to the point that they become new standards.

In order to implement a CE, companies can introduce practices such as energy saving, increasing the efficiency of materials in production processes, designing less resource-consuming products, decreasing waste and facilitating waste management. These practices could involve inputting a considerable amount of recycled materials in the production process, utilising waste as material in the production process or utilising waste to power combustion generators, utilising a considerable amount of energy from renewable sources or energy entirely from renewable sources, using electric or hybrid vehicles for transport, searching for the least emitting means of goods and service transport in the delivery process, taking advantage of internal remains and residues in production processes and the operations of other companies.

Companies, local governments and grant institutions can incentivise change by introducing environmental criteria in purchasing, construction, production and other operations. For example, they can include obligations to purchase recycled raw materials, to buy environmentally certified products or to use biodegradable, reusable, recyclable or remanufacturable materials. Green public procurement is becoming a tool more often used (EC, 2008, 2015, 2021, EEA, 2019), with recommendations and criteria set by the EC (GPP Criteria and Requirements (europa.eu), accessed 10.09.2023). Common EU green public procurement criteria were developed in a process led by the Joint Research Centre involving a stakeholder advisory group, and they can be incorporated in public procurement procedures for goods, services or works in order to reduce the environmental impact of purchases. The criteria are voluntary, and they concern procurement of cleaning products and services, computers, monitors, tablets and smartphones, data centres, server rooms and cloud services, electricity, food catering services and vending machines, furniture, imaging equipment, consumables and print services, office building design, construction and management.

It should be widely recognised by all actors in the market that in an environmentally conscientious society companies are competing with the highest product quality, but also with actual and communicated sustainability (without greenwashing, which is more and more often traced and recognised), participation in CE networks, innovation and green/sustainable business models leading to lower costs.

In view of the above, a successful change from a linear to a CE is ensured by all actors being involved in leading the transition. Key stakeholders include local governments, companies and society. The transition can be enabled by financing CE practices or projects, as well as by promoting the use of local resources, synergies in the local economy and by demonstrating and promoting sustainable energy uses. In addition, awareness-raising campaigns, education and advisory services are important to engage in transformative processes from a linear to a CE.

Examples of CE initiatives are as follows:

- packaging return systems for reuse/waste with incentives;
- developing bike lending systems;
- electric vehicle rental systems;
- increasing green spaces in the city;
- developing markets for second-hand goods;
- developing local fresh produce markets;
- implementing systems for reuse of water;
- implementing energy efficiency measures;
- creating a municipal CE office as a catalyst for initiatives;
- waste generation payment systems.

Local initiatives helping to boost and mainstream a CE locally are as follows:

- developing training and awareness campaigns (e.g., encouraging recycling);
- ensuring that there is a market niche/need for the development of CE initiatives;
- creating technical advisory committees for new initiatives;
- developing new circular business models;
- adapting and/or creating appropriate regulations (e.g., on organic waste recycling and public purchasing);
- encouraging use of by-products by companies;
- involving citizens;
- facilitating and financially supporting companies that promote circular projects (e.g., with tax exemptions);

- coordinating different local initiatives (also regional, national and European ones);
- limiting bureaucracy.

Practices that citizens and companies can adopt for the success of the CE are as follows:

- consuming more local products;
- consuming greener products;
- reducing water consumption;
- reducing energy consumption;
- using the car less;
- separating waste,
- taking waste to an authorised management point;
- trying to repair more;
- using more second-hand products.

Barriers preventing or hindering company transitions towards a CE model include the following:

- difficulty in changing the linear consumption model from using and throwing away to a circular model in which reuse prevails;
- lack of awareness in society;
- lack of information of society;
- lack of interest in society;
- limited product information for consumers;
- lack of an urgent need to change the economic model;
- the CE insufficiently promoted by the administration;
- insufficient and/or not adapted legislation;
- difficulty in accessing financing;
- over complex bureaucracy;
- insufficient technology and eco-design (e.g., most products have not been designed to be recycled, reused and/or recovered).

## 1.4 Circular economy implementation in word economies and mapping CE networks

A vast amount of scientific literature has studied CE issues so far, in both scientific and application domains, in relation to national markets and local case studies (regions, cities and companies) in various sectors, for a variety of products and services and their supply chains. Several examples are presented below.

Bocken et al. (2017) addressed the complexity of CE literature in recent years and indicate emerging issues such as environmental benefits of CE practices; social, economic and political factors in successful implementation of

CE strategies; scalability of CE strategies and how more advanced CE strategies beyond recycling can be adopted by businesses.

A very interesting review of CE implementation worldwide (Ghisellini et al., 2016) indicates that although in China the CE is promoted as a top-down national political objective, in other places like the EU, Japan and the United States, it is instead a tool to design bottom-up environmental and waste management policies. The study shows that worldwide implementation of the CE is still in the early stages and mainly focused on recycling rather than reuse. In some sectors, in particular in waste management, large waste recycling rates are achieved in certain developed countries. In particular, Ghisellini et al. (2016) point out that in 2010, average municipal solid waste generation rates per capita were at the level of 720 kg in the USA, 512 kg in European Union Member States, 380 kg in Japan and 250 kg in China, whereas industrial waste collection rates were about 90% in developed countries and 67% in China. They also indicate that the involvement of all actors in society and their capacity to link and create suitable collaboration and exchange patterns are pivotal in the transition to a CE. Company and investor motivation should be ensured by economic returns on investment (Ghisellini et al., 2016).

Understanding the drivers of the transition from a linear to a CE is the subject of research on both the supply side of the market, including producers and distribution networks (e.g., Domenech et al., 2019; Gue et al., 2020), and the demand side – consumers and their choices (Klimkiewicz et al., 2023).

A few papers have analysed and mapped interrelationships among CE transition drivers from the perspectives of different sectors. For instance, Domenech et al. (2019) mapped industrial symbiosis networks in the EU with an average size of the mapped networks of approximately 473 members and a median of approximately 100 members. They determined that the geographical scope of the synergies is dependent on the type of waste stream, waste by-products, transport costs and the market value of secondary materials. The obstacles to industrial symbiosis development in Europe identified are 'weakness of economic incentives given the low margin of industrial symbiosis projects associated with undeveloped secondary markets, geographical variation of incentives and drivers, given differences in policy frameworks and support mechanisms (e.g., landfill tax levels) and legislative issues that make transport over geographical boundaries extremely complex and administratively burdensome' (Domenech et al., 2019). Gue et al. (2020) presented a methodological framework for mapping causality networks for a macro-level transition towards a CE based on sector perceptions. The study uses a fuzzy DEMATEL model to quantify linguistic inputs. This procedure allows drivers to be characterised as causes or effects based on their position in the causality network. The work presents a case study of the Philippines as an example of a developing country CE transition.

Klimkiewicz et al. (2023), in their study, dealt with the issue of designing an eco-friendly hierarchy of remedies in consumer sales law. They designed a method for calculating the environmental impacts of legislative provisions based on the Life Cycle Thinking and Life Cycle Assessment methods used to compare different remedy scenarios when the consumer chooses repair, replacement, price reduction or termination. They also tackled the issue of durability, as it is an important factor in encouraging sustainable consumption (Sun et al., 2021), but its impact varies depending on the product category (Cooper & Gutowski, 2017).

Municipal and local government studies are more frequent than small and medium enterprise-related applications. Based on a review of 126 academic papers indexed in Scopus, Ferasso et al. (2023) indicated that although CEs in larger businesses and multinational corporations have been well studied, the transformation of SMEs towards circularity has not been well addressed. Vahidzadeh et al. (2021) analysed 112 Scopus-index papers on regional industrial symbiosis and found that the main subtopics are regional learning, waste minimisation, assessment, urban-industrial symbiosis and Life Cycle Thinking, energy efficiency, operational carriers and social issues. Ferasso et al. (2020) studied 253 articles from the Scopus Web of Science and ScienceDirect scientific databases and showed that current topics in CE publications are business models, the CE, circular business models, value, supply chains, transitions, resources, waste and reuse.

A few examples of national, regional and municipal studies are presented below.

Dagilienė et al. (2021) investigated whether and how local governments contribute to the CE in Lithuania and discovered that CE solutions, which are not regulated, are very weakly implemented locally and that the current solutions are mostly orientated to waste management. They found that local governments should be more proactive and strengthen networking with local businesses along the value chain.

Christensen et al. (2022) developed a study of the creation, potential and barriers to a closed-loop production and consumption value chain on Bornholm Island in Denmark. Positive business cases for recycling are identified. The study concludes that uniform products such as bricks are more likely to become viable business models than other materials, due to their low volume, lack of uniformity and relatively inconsistent quality.

The economic, environmental and social feasibility of a CE in relation to municipal solid waste management is studied by Rathore and Sarmah (2020). A case study of Bilaspur city in India presents the environmental benefits of carbon emission reduction due to utilisation of collected organic waste by converting it into biogas and then using it as fuel in a thermal power plant as an alternative to using coal.

An overview of selected SME- and business-related studies is presented below.

Dey et al. (2020) surveyed 130 randomly selected SMEs in the Midlands of the United Kingdom in order to identify issues, challenges and opportunities involved in adopting a CE in SMEs. Based on a literature review and four case studies, Geissdoerfer et al. (2018) proposed a framework to integrate various (in their complexity and value proposition) circular business models and circular supply chains in different loops: closing loops, slowing loops, intensifying loops, narrowing loops and dematerialising loops. Holzer et al. (2021) studied 183 SMEs in Austria and revealed that efficient use of resources and procurement of resources play a major role for Austrian SMEs. The companies in the study are clustered into four strategic groups: CE frontrunners, fast followers, a late majority and laggards. This classification could be helpful for policymakers, intermediaries and cluster representatives in facilitating a shift towards a CE.

Sectoral studies have also been conducted. Examples of agriculture, building and construction, pulp and paper, pharmaceutical industries and bio-plastics are given below.

There are many examples of CE initiatives undertaken by agriculture companies, for example, the Spanish Agricultura y Conservas S.A. at its establishment in Algemesí is involved in a project that consists of reusing shell citrus for the production of pellets (unpublished empirical research by Segui (2023)).

Building and construction sector CE is studied by Norouzi et al. (2021) in a literature review. They found three main domains of CE studies in this sector, which are as follows:

- energy and energy efficiency in buildings;
- recycling, waste management and alternative construction materials;
- sustainable development.

Ferreira et al. (2019) studied the Portuguese pulp and paper sector and showed that central organisation, sand producers and end users of material mixtures are the entities most powerful in the symbiosis network.

Tsolakis et al. (2023) conducted value chain mapping of the US pharmaceutical industry in order to explore potential supply network configurations utilising microalgae feedstocks and found that smart renewable-feedstock technologies are crucial for sustainable network design.

Finally, bio-based plastics are attracting increasing attention due to their perceived sustainability and circularity. A rapidly growing market in them will lead to bio-based plastics being responsible for a significant proportion of plastic waste. Regarding this, Ritzen et al. (2023) highlighted that the ability to recover a plastic not only depends on the composition of the plastic but also on the way a product is designed.

## References

Aven, T. (2020). Climate change risk – What is it and how should it be expressed? *Journal of Risk Research*, *23*(11), 1387–1404.

Ayres, R. U., & Kneese, A. V. (1969). Production, consumption, and externalities. *The American Economic Review*, *59*(3), 282–297.

Benyus, J. M. (2002). *Biomimicry*. New York: Harper Perennial.

Bocken, N. M. P., Olivetti, E. A., Cullen, J. M., Potting, J., & Lifset, R. (2017). Taking the circularity to the next level: A special issue on the circular economy. *Journal of Industrial Ecology*, *21*(3), 476–482. https://doi.org/10.1111/JIEC.12606

Brocchi, D. (2010). The cultural dimension of Un/sustainability. In S. Bergmann & D. Gerten (Eds.), *Religion and Dangerous Environmental Change: Transdisciplinary Perspectives on the Ethics of Climate and Sustainability*, 145–176. Studies on Religion and the Environment 2. Berlin and London: Lit.

Carter, C. R., & Rogers, D. S. (2008). A framework of sustainable supply chain management: Moving toward new theory. *International Journal of Physical Distribution & Logistics Management*, *38*(5), 360–387.

Christensen, T. B., Johansen, M. R., Buchard, M. V., & Glarborg, C. N. (2022). Closing the material loops for construction and demolition waste: The circular economy on the island Bornholm, Denmark. *Resources, Conservation & Recycling Advances*, *15*, 200104. https://doi.org/10.1016/J.RCRADV.2022.200104

Clune, W. H., & Zehnder, A. J. B. (2020). The evolution of sustainability models, from descriptive to strategic, to the three pillars framework for applied solutions. *Sustainability Science*, *15*(do), 1001–1006. https://doi.org/10.1007/s11625-019-00776-8

Considine, T. J., & Larson, D. F. (2006). The environment as a factor of production. *Journal of Environmental Economics and Management*, *52*(3), 645–662.

Cooper, D. R., & Gutowski, T. G. (2017). The environmental impacts of reuse: A review. *Journal of Industrial Ecology*, *21*(1), 38–56. https://doi.org/10.1111/JIEC.12388

Dagilienė, L., Varaniūtė, V., & Bruneckienė, J. (2021). Local governments' perspective on implementing the circular economy: A framework for future solutions. *Journal of Cleaner Production*, *310*, 127340. https://doi.org/10.1016/J.JCLEPRO.2021.127340

Dey, P. K., Malesios, C., De, D., Budhwar, P., Chowdhury, S., & Cheffi, W. (2020). Circular economy to enhance sustainability of small and medium-sized enterprises. *Business Strategy and the Environment*, *29*(6), 2145–2169. https://doi.org/10.1002/BSE.2492

Directive 2014/95/EU of the European Parliament and of the Council of 22 October 2014 amending Directive 2013/34/EU as regards disclosure of non-financial and diversity information by certain large undertakings and groups Text with EEA relevance, EUR-Lex - 32014L0095 - EN - EUR-Lex (europa.eu).

Directive (EU) 2022/2464 of the European Parliament and of the Council of 14 December 2022 amending Regulation (EU) No 537/2014, Directive 2004/109/EC, Directive 2006/43/EC and Directive 2013/34/EU, as regards corporate sustainability reporting, EUR-Lex - 32022L2464 - EN - EUR-Lex (europa.eu).

Domenech, T., Bleischwitz, R., Doranova, A., Panayotopoulos, D., & Roman, L. (2019). Mapping industrial symbiosis development in Europe_ typologies of networks, characteristics, performance and contribution to the circular economy. *Resources, Conservation and Recycling*, *141*, 76–98. https://doi.org/10.1016/J.RESCONREC.2018.09.016

Duraiappah, A. K., Asah, S. T., Brondizio, E. S., Kosoy, N., O'Farrell, P. J., Prieur-Richard, A. H., Subramanian, S. M., & Takeuchi, K. (2014). Managing the mismatches to provide ecosystem services for human well-being: A conceptual framework for understanding the new commons. *Current Opinion in Environmental Sustainability*, *7*, 94–100. https://doi.org/10.1016/j.cosust.2013.11.031

European Commission (EC). (2011). Communication from the Commission to the European Parliament, the Council, the European Economic and Social Committee and the Committee of the Regions. A renewed EU strategy 2011-14 for Corporate Social Responsibility. COM(2011) 681 final.

European Commission (EC). (2008). Communication from the Commission to the European Parliament, the Council, the European Economic and Social Committee and the Committee of the Regions. Public procurement for a better environment, COM/2008/0400.

European Commission (EC). (2015). Public Procurement Indicators 2013. These figures exclude spending by utility companies; earlier estimates (2011).

European Commission (EC). (2017). Communication from the Commission to the European Parliament, the Council, the European Economic and Social Committee and the Committee of the Regions, the role of waste-to-energy in the circular economy, Brussels, 26.01.2017, COM/2017/034 final, eur-lex.europa.eu/legal-content/EN/TXT/PDF/?uri=CELEX:52017DC0034

European Commission (EC). (2018a). Communication from the Commission to the European Parliament, the Council, the European Economic and Social Committee and the Committee of the Regions on a monitoring framework for the circular economy, Strasbourg, 16.01.2018, COM/2018/029 final, eur-lex.europa.eu/legal-content/EN/TXT/PDF/?uri=CELEX:52018DC0029

European Commission (EC). (2018b). Communication from the Commission to the European Parliament, the Council, the European Economic and Social Committee and the Committee of the Regions on the implementation of the circular economy package: options to address the interface between chemical, product and waste legislation (Text with EEA relevance) options to address the interface between chemical, product and waste legislation, Strasbourg, 16.01.2018, COM/2018/032 final. https://eur-lex.europa.eu/legal-content/EN/TXT/PDF/?uri=CELEX:52018DC0032

European Commission (EC) (2018c). Communication from the Commission to the European Parliament, the Council, the European Economic and Social Committee and the Committee of the Regions, a European Strategy for Plastics in a Circular Economy, Brussels, 16.01.2018, COM/2018/028 final. https://eur-lex.europa.eu/resource.html?uri=cellar:2df5d1d2-fac7-11e7-b8f5-01aa75ed71a1.0001.02/DOC_1&format=PDF

European Commission (EC). (2018d). ANNEXES to the Communication from the Commission to the European Parliament, the Council, the European Economic and Social Committee and the Committee of the Regions A European Strategy for Plastics in a Circular Economy, Brussels, 16.01.2018. https://eur-lex.europa.eu/resource.html?uri=cellar:2df5d1d2-fac7-11e7-b8f5-01aa75ed71a1.0001.02/DOC_2&format=PDF

European Commission (EC). (2019). Report from the Commission to the European Parliament, the Council, the European Economic and Social Committee and the Committee of the Regions on the implementation of the Circular Economy Action Plan, Brussels, 04.03.2019, COM(2019)190 final. https://eur-lex.europa.eu/legal-content/EN/TXT/PDF/?uri=CELEX:52019DC0190

European Commission (EC). (2021). Commission Notice, Guidance on Innovation Procurement, Brussels, 18.6.2021, C(2021)4320.

European Environment Agency (EEA). (2019). *The European Environment State and Outlook 2020 Knowledge for Transition to a Sustainable Europe*. Luxembourg: EEA.

Ellen MacArthur Foundation. (2012). Circular Economy Report – Towards the Circular Economy, t.1, Towards the Circular Economy (mckinsey.com), accessed 15.09.2023.

Ferasso, M., Beliaeva, T., Kraus, S., Clauss, T., & Ribeiro-Soriano, D. (2020). Circular economy business models: The state of research and avenues ahead. *Business Strategy and the Environment*, *29*(8), 3006–3024. https://doi.org/10.1002/BSE.2554

Ferasso, M., Tortato, U., & Ikram, M. (2023). Mapping the circular economy in the small and medium-sized enterprises field: An exploratory network analysis. *Cleaner and Responsible Consumption*, *11*, 100149. https://doi.org/10.1016/J.CLRC.2023.100149

Ferreira, I. A., Barreiros, M. S., & Carvalho, H. (2019). The industrial symbiosis network of the biomass fluidized bed boiler sand – Mapping its value network. *Resources, Conservation and Recycling*, *149*, 595–604. https://doi.org/10.1016/J.RESCONREC.2019.06.024

Finkbeiner, M., Schau, E. M., Lehmann, A., & Traverso, M. (2010). Towards life cycle sustainability assessment. *Sustainability*, *2*(10), 3309–3322.

FOB. (2022). Raport Dobre Praktyki CSR. [Report Good Practices of CSR.] Forum Odpowiedzialnego Biznesu. Warszawa.

Geissdoerfer, M., Morioka, S. N., de Carvalho, M. M., & Evans, S. (2018). Business models and supply chains for the circular economy. *Journal of Cleaner Production*, *190*, 712–721. https://doi.org/10.1016/j.jclepro.2018.04.159

Geissdoerfer, M., Savaget, P., Bocken, N. M. P., & Hultink, E. J. (2017). The circular economy – A new sustainability paradigm? *Journal of Cleaner Production*, *143*, 757–768. https://doi.org/10.1016/j.jclepro.2016.12.048

Ghisellini, P., Cialani, C., & Ulgiati, S. (2016). A review on circular economy: The expected transition to a balanced interplay of environmental and economic systems. *Journal of Cleaner Production*, *114*, 11–32. https://doi.org/10.1016/j.jclepro.2015.09.007

Graedel, T. E., & Allenby, B. R. (1995). *Industrial Ecology*. Englewood Cliffs, NJ: Prentice Hall.

Gue, I. H. V., Promentilla, M. A. B., Tan, R. R., & Ubando, A. T. (2020). Sector perception of circular economy driver interrelationships. *Journal of Cleaner Production*, *276*, 123204. https://doi.org/10.1016/J.JCLEPRO.2020.123204

Harvard Business School online. The Triple Bottom Line: What It Is & Why It's Important (hbs.edu), accessed 15.09.2023.

Hickel, J. (2021). What does degrowth mean? A few points of clarification, *Globalizations*, *18*(7), 1105–1111. https://doi.org/10.1080/14747731.2020.1812222

Holzer, D., Rauter, R., Fleiß, E., & Stern, T. (2021). Mind the gap: Towards a systematic circular economy encouragement of small and medium-sized companies. *Journal of Cleaner Production*, *298*, 126696. https://doi.org/10.1016/j.jclepro.2021.126696

IRP, S. B., Ramaswami, A., Schandl, H., O'Brien, M., Pelton, R., Acquatella, J., & Giljum, S. (2017). Assessing Global Resource Use: A Systems Approach to Resource Efficiency and Pollution Reduction. *UN Environment, Nairobi*.

Kallis, G. (2017). Radical dematerialization and degrowth. *Philosophical Transactions of the Royal Society A: Mathematical, Physical and Engineering Sciences*, *375*(2095), 20160383. https://doi.org/10.1098/rsta.2016.0383

Kallis, G., et al. (2018). Research on degrowth. *Annual Review of Environment and Resources, 43*(1), 291–316. https://doi.org/10.1146/annurev-environ-102017-025941

Khmara, Y., & Kronenberg, J. (2018). Degrowth in business: An oxymoron or a viable business model for sustainability? *Journal of Cleaner Production, 177*: 721–731. https://doi.org/10.1016/j.jclepro.2017.12.182

Kirchherr, J., Yang, N. H. N., Schulze-Spüntrup, F., Heerink, M. J., & Hartley, K. (2023). Conceptualizing the circular economy (revisited): An analysis of 221 definitions. *Resources, Conservation and Recycling, 194*, 107001. https://doi.org/10.1016/J.RESCONREC.2023.107001

Klimkiewicz, K., Dubel, A., & Południak-Gierz, K. (2023). Supporting environmentally conscious consumer sales law by life-cycle thinking. *Contemporary Economics, 17*(2), 174–196. https://doi.org/10.5709/ce.1897-9254.505

Leal Filho, W., Tripathi, S. K., Andrade Guerra, J. B. S. O. D., Giné-Garriga, R., Orlovic Lovren, V., & Willats, J. (2019). Using the sustainable development goals towards a better understanding of sustainability challenges. *International Journal of Sustainable Development & World Ecology, 26*(2), 179–190.

Leontief, W. (1991). The economy as a circular flow. *Structural Change and Economic Dynamics, 2*(1), 181–212.

Lyle, J. T. (1994). *Regenerative Design for Sustainable Development*. New York: John Wiley & Sons.

Mair, J., & Marti, I. (2006). Social Entrepreneurship Research: A Source of Explanation, Prediction and Delight. University of Illinois at Urbana-Champaign's Academy for Entrepreneurial Leadership Historical Research Reference in Entrepreneurship, SSRN: https://ssrn.com/abstract=1502011

McDonough, W., & Braungart, M. (2010). Cradle to Cradle: Remaking the Way We Make Things, Farrar, Straus and Giroux, New York.

Meadows, D. H., Meadows, D. L., Randers, J., Behrens, I. I. I., & William, W. (1972). *The Limits to Growth: A Report for the Club of Rome's Project on the Predicament of Mankind*. New York: Universe Books. ISBN 0876631650.

Meadows, D. H., Meadows, D. L., & Randers, J. (1992). Beyond The Limits to Growth.

Mebratu, D. (2001). The knowledge dimension of the sustainability challenge. *International Journal of Economic Development, 3*(1),1–21.

Michalak, D., Rosiek, K., & Szyja, P. (2020). *Gospodarka niskoemisyjna, gospodarka cyrkularna, zielona gospodarka*. Łódź: Wyd. Uniwersytetu Łódzkiego.

Mollison, B., & Holmgren, D. (1978). *Permaculture One: A Perennial Agriculture for Human Settlements*. Melbourne, Australia: Transworld Publishers.

Norouzi, M., Chàfer, M., Cabeza, L. F., Jiménez, L., & Boer, D. (2021). Circular economy in the building and construction sector: A scientific evolution analysis. *Journal of Building Engineering, 44*, 102704. https://doi.org/10.1016/J.JOBE.2021.102704

Organisation for Economic Co-operation and Development (OECD). (2017). *Green Growth Indicators 2017*. Paris: OECD Publishing.

Ozili, P. K. (2021). Circular economy, banks, and other financial Institutions: What's in it for them? *Circular Economy and Sustainability, 1*(3), 787–798.

Ozili, P. K. (2022). Sustainability and sustainable development research around the world. *Managing Global Transitions, 20*(3), 259–293. https://doi.org/10.26493/1854-6935.20.259-293

Pamučar, D., Durán-Romero, G., Yazdani, M., & López, A. M. (2023). A decision analysis model for smart mobility system development under circular economy approach. *Socio-Economic Planning Sciences, 86*, 101474. https://doi.org/10.1016/j.seps.2022.101474

Pauli, G. A. (2010). *The Blue Economy: 10 Years, 100 Innovations, 100 Million Jobs*. Taos, NM: Paradigm Publications.

Pearce, D., Markandya, A., & Barbier, E. B. (1989). *Blueprint for a Green Economy*. London: Earthscan.

Porter, M. E., & van der Linde, C. (1995). Green and competitive: Ending the stalemate. *Harvard Business Review*, *73*(5), 120–134.

Przygodzki, Z. (2022). Policy Framework and Market analysis. Policy Model – Territorial Ecosystem Framework for Circular Economy in Lodzkie Region, Raport Frontsh1p, Łódź.

Purvis, A., et al. (2020). Status & Trends – Nature, Chapter 2.2 of the IPBES Global Assessment of Biodiversity and Ecosystem Services, Intergovernmental Panel on Biodiversity and Ecosystem Services, IPBES.

Rathore, P., & Sarmah, S. P. (2020). Economic, environmental and social optimization of solid waste management in the context of circular economy. *Computers & Industrial Engineering*, *145*, 106510. https://doi.org/10.1016/J.CIE.2020.106510

Ritzen, L., Sprecher, B., Bakker, C., & Balkenende, R. (2023). Bio-based plastics in a circular economy: A review of recovery pathways and implications for product design. *Resources, Conservation and Recycling*, *199*, 107268. https://doi.org/10.1016/J.RESCONREC.2023.107268

Sanyé-Mengual, E., Secchi, M., Corrado, S., Beylot, A., & Sala, S. (2019). Assessing the decoupling of economic growth from environmental impacts in the European Union: A consumption-based approach. *Journal of Cleaner Production*, *236*, 117535. https://doi.org/10.1016/j.jclepro.2019.07.010

Schöggl, J. P., Stumpf, L., & Baumgartner, R. J. (2020). The narrative of sustainability and circular economy – A longitudinal review of two decades of research. *Resources, Conservation and Recycling*, *163*, 105073. https://doi.org/10.1016/J.RESCONREC.2020.105073

Stahel, W. (2010). *The Performance Economy*. Basingstoke, New York: Palgrave MacMillan.

Segui, A. (2023). Autors' interview with Antoni Segui, professor at the University of Valencia, Spain, on 30.06.2023.

Stojanović, I., Ateljević, J., & Stević, R. S. (2016). Good governance as a tool of sustainable development. *European Journal of Sustainable Development*, *5*(4), 558–573.

Sun, J. J., Bellezza, S., & Paharia, N. (2021). Buy less, buy luxury: Understanding and overcoming product durability neglect for sustainable consumption. *Journal of Marketing*, *85*(3), 28–43. https://doi.org/10.1177/0022242921993172

TEEB. (2010). *The Economics of Ecosystems and Biodiversity Ecological and Economic Foundations*. P. Kumar (Ed.). London and Washington: Earthscan.

Trainer, T. (2012). De-growth: Do you realise what it means? *Futures*, *44*(6), 590–599. https://doi.org/10.1016/j.futures.2012.03.020

Tsolakis, N., Goldsmith, A. T., Aivazidou, E., & Kumar, M. (2023). Microalgae-based circular supply chain configurations using industry 4.0 technologies for pharmaceuticals. *Journal of Cleaner Production*, *395*, 136397. https://doi.org/10.1016/J.JCLEPRO.2023.136397

United Nations, General Assembly (UN). (1987). Report of the World Commission on Environment and Development. Annex: Our Common Future, Forty-second session. Item 83 (e) of the provisional agenda, A/42/427.

United Nations General Assembly (UN). (2015). Transforming our world: The 2030 Agenda for Sustainable Development, Resolution adopted by the General Assembly on 25 September 201 (A/RES/70/1).

Vahidzadeh, R., Bertanza, G., Sbaffoni, S., & Vaccari, M. (2021). Regional industrial symbiosis: A review based on social network analysis. *Journal of Cleaner Production*, *280*, 124054. https://doi.org/10.1016/J.JCLEPRO.2020.124054

Wackernagel, M., Hanscom, L., & Lin, D. (2017). Making the sustainable development goals consistent with sustainability. *Frontiers in Energy Research*, *5*, 18, 1–5. https://doi.org/10.3389/fenrg.2017.00018

# 2 The evolution of sustainable marketing against a background of selected market changes

## 2.1 The evolution of the conventional understanding of marketing

In the past, there was an accepted belief that marketing and sustainability were distinct concepts. Until recently, marketing was commonly associated with generating demand and convincing customers to purchase more (Nagy et al., 2012). However, the modern role of marketing is much more profound (Kitchen & Burgmann, 2015; Kitchen & Proctor, 2015). Changes in the marketing orientation of companies observed over the years have caused the approach to marketing to change. In the early 1950s, the market became interested in the needs of consumers – the product was supposed to be the answer to those needs (Silva et al., 2020). According to the marketing orientation of the market, the aim of marketing (and of whole enterprises) is to meet needs in a way that makes a profit (Powell & Osborne, 2015). This is possible by selecting and analysing the right market, learning about the target group and its needs and building a competitive advantage (Gregor & Kalicińska-Kula, 2014; Hansen, 1973). However, an increase in the explosive growth of supply, and thus competition in the market, and the drive to maximise corporate profits has led marketing to be equated with a set of techniques and tools for generating demand, increasing sales and convincing customers to buy products they do not need (Taranko, 2015; Wiktor, 2002). The increase in the intensity of promotional activities persuaded consumers to maximise purchases of products (Kozielski, 2011). This allowed companies to maximise their revenue in the short term. This was the primary aim of company managers, whose bonuses and salaries depended on the financial performance of their companies at the end of the year or quarter (Zawadzka, 2006). Therefore, they were often not interested in investing in technologies with a very long payback period or which were only associated with reducing the negative impact of the company on the environment rather than affecting its profitability.

However, the rapid increase in the supply of products and the associated greater competition, together with the development of a range of management tools, made this approach gradually less profitable and it began to be

DOI: 10.4324/9781003408642-3

negatively perceived socially. There was a need to organise marketing activities and redefine their goals (Bruhn & Schnebelen, 2017). This coincided with the emergence of the concept of marketing 2.0, which was a result of the evolution and development of communication and information technologies. The challenges that companies faced resulted from the fact that consumers were much better informed and could search for and compare information about similar products and services (Priest et al., 2013). Consumers also became better informed and more demanding in evaluating the performance of companies (Siuda, 2012). Technological advances and the development of computerisation and the internet made it easier for consumers to access more information that helped them see, assess and react to the practices of companies (Finne & Grönroos, 2017). The media, environmental and consumer organisations and government administrations reported on hostile and irresponsible business activities. In the marketing field, the concept of marketing 3.0 emerged. This period was referred to as the era of value. This stage evolved from treating individuals as simple consumers to treating them as human beings with minds, hearts and feelings. In this period, companies facing the deepest needs and desires of consumers must adapt their marketing and communication strategies to identify, create and deliver value not only from an economic, functional or environmental point of view but spiritual and sentimental issues began to matter (Mirońska, 2010). Greater sensitivity to consumers and consideration of the impact of emotions on their purchasing process forced businesses to analyse the factors affecting consumer decisions (Thaler, 2009). This analysis led to the emergence of social and holistic marketing. Both concepts emphasise the complexity of factors influencing the market behaviour of consumers. Purchasing decisions are influenced by consumers' experiences and extensive knowledge of how producers operate in the market. In addition to production activities, social responsibility, activism for society and employees and a sustainable approach to doing business matter.

When creating marketing strategies, companies began to seek a balance between three factors: company profits, consumer desires and social interest (Brandys, 2013). It was decided to curb the misallocation of resources resulting from the production of products created in the minds of designers without consulting potential customers. It quickly became apparent that too many offerings that did not meet customer expectations despite huge promotional expenditures were not finding buyers in the market. Attempts had already been made to redefine how a company organises its work and to define the needs of buyers as the starting point of a typical production process. However, it turned out that although at the theoretical level this sounds very attractive in practice, it is challenging to implement. The first problem is how potential customers define their needs (Karjaluoto et al., 2015). They cannot create new solutions and anticipate the benefits of acquiring them. Despite many services to support them in the sales process, today's customers do not always choose the offers most beneficial to themselves. It is challenging to select an offer which will be advantageous to the buyer in the long term. It will satisfy current desires and not harm the customer's environment (Sun et al., 2022). This approach is becoming a necessity because nowadays more and more people are buying more and more products, with the result that the impact of these purchases on the climate and the human environment is growing (Khan et al., 2021). Scientists argue that stopping some negative environmental processes is possible provided that purchases and the associated misallocation of natural resources and overproduction of waste are reduced (Semprebon et al., 2019). Increasing awareness of adverse changes in the environment and the growing dangers resulting from this make it increasingly common to generate pro-environmental behaviour that will help stop negative phenomena occurring in the environment. This belief sparked the emergence of sustainable development and led to marketing interest in the achievements of sustainability science (Jaiswal et al., 2022; Zavali & Theodoropoulou, 2018).

## 2.2 The beginnings of sustainable marketing and the green supply chain

For some marketers, the history of sustainable marketing began in 1982 with the publication of Naisbitt (1982). Back then, the interest of marketing in environmental issues was considered one of the megatrends that would shape surrounding reality. The interest in this topic led to environmental issues being considered a tool for improving the competitive situation of companies operating in the market (Corrado et al., 2021). Consumer interest in environmentally friendly purchases led to the emergence of green marketing, a response to the need to implement green practices and resulting market needs (Kumar Kar & Harichandan, 2022). Initially, it was a response to the drawbacks of traditional marketing and the resulting environmental risks (Honkanen & Young, 2015). Companies used the environmental campaigns they implemented to promote their businesses. Only later did green marketing begin to evolve (Nagy et al., 2012).

Environmental marketing is defined differently in the literature. This is due to the different approaches of companies to environmental issues and to the environmental awareness of consumers. An overview of sample concepts for interpreting green marketing can be found in Brandys (2013):

- Ecological marketing is a system of knowledge, skills and rules of conduct that enables participants in the emerging market of ecological goods and services to meet their needs and achieve success. It can be used by companies with a clarified strategy of sustainable development and aimed at an identified group of ecological consumers with the support of state environmental policy or that of a group of states (Bronakowski, 1997, p. 66).

- Eco-marketing is a set of integrated practices to identify and satisfy customer needs profitably and more effectively than competitors, to achieve mutual satisfaction and simultaneously ensure social sustainability (Sieńko, 2000).
- Environmental marketing is the process of identifying, anticipating and meeting the needs of individual customers and society as a whole in a profitable way while ensuring environmental sustainability (Peattie, 1995).
- Environmental marketing is a social and managerial process in which specific individuals and groups get what they need and want by creating, offering and exchanging goods that have ecological value (Białoń, 1998).
- Ecological marketing is the process of satisfying the needs of consumers and society by planning and realising the concepts, pricing, promotion and distribution of ideas, goods and services in a way that satisfies the exchange participants and at the same time is ecological (Zaremba-Warnke, 2000).

Green marketing is otherwise known as eco-marketing, environmental marketing and ecologically responsible marketing. In various works, these terms appear interchangeably, and for the purposes of this chapter, they are assumed to describe the same phenomenon. A closely related expression which is used in this work is sustainable marketing, which is a broader concept than green marketing. It is described more extensively later in this chapter.

Some of the primary areas of green marketing practice are as follows:

- abandoning animal testing;
- responsible waste management;
- using biodegradable materials and reducing the production of harmful and hazardous waste;
- countering irresponsible and excessive consumption;
- rational use of energy, including renewable sources;
- eliminating from the composition of products substances that are harmful to the health of consumers (such as refined fats, sweeteners and preservatives);
- seeking innovations that modify the lifestyles of consumers (Marek & Jerzyk, 2018).

These practices were not initially driven by altruistic motives guiding the behaviour of companies. They responded to consumer expectations and were aimed at improving company reputations. A category of green goods and services has been identified, that is, ones that can be considered environmentally friendly (manufacture and/or use of them is carried out with environmental considerations in mind) (Kamiński, 2019). This information is of great interest in many markets. Nevertheless, at the same time, it is common to look at consumers' environmental decisions through the prisms of their economic viability, improved health and safety. Therefore, some pro-environmental behaviours are more popular than others (Lisowski et al., 2022). For example, consumers reduce electricity consumption because it is associated with clear savings (and is pro-environmental, by the way), while restrictions on water consumption no longer provide such savings. Therefore, consumers are not so convinced of the need for them (Lisowski et al., 2021).

As the world's population grows and production and consumption expand, the number of negative phenomena that threaten the livelihood of future generations is also increasing (Inieke, 2021). This is leading to increased awareness of the need to make changes in the operation of the global economy. For entrepreneurs, being aware of the growing importance of environmental issues in the economy, reducing the environmental impact of business activities, considering all the links in supply chains and considering the interconnections and interactions between them and the natural environment is becoming an increasingly important challenge. This comprehensive approach makes it possible to take adequate measures to protect the environment while at the same time increasing opportunities for eco-innovative solutions (Ryszko, 2014). These expectations are being met by the increasing prevalence of green supply chain management. According to Hervani et al. (2005), green supply chain management includes green procurement, green manufacturing and materials management, green distribution and marketing and reverse logistics. For Shang et al. (2010), the process consists of green manufacturing and packaging, participatory environmental management, green marketing, green procurement, green resource and inventory management and eco-design. In this process, Ryszko (2007, pp. 73–83) distinguishes the following features:

- Pro-environmental product (or service) design and development, taking into account a holistic view of the environmental impact of the product in all phases of its life, focusing on continual improvement of the eco-efficiency of the product;
- Pro-environmental sourcing/purchasing. In this stage it will be necessary, among other things, to take into account the ecological characteristics of raw materials when purchasing them, to minimise the environmental impact of transporting raw materials and to use reusable and recyclable packaging;
- Environmentally friendly manufacturing. The priority of production planning and control is to reduce the consumption of raw materials and energy and the generation of pollution, taking into account reuse of the resulting post-production waste on-site (internal recycling) or off-site (external recycling);
- Green marketing (also referred to in the literature as eco marketing and environmental marketing), informing the company's stakeholders about the green features of products and environmental responsibility, and stimulating demand for products and services that have less environmental impact;

- Pro-environmental distribution, related to the manufacturer's extended responsibility for selecting the means of transport and distribution channels that are least harmful to the environment, and eco-friendly packaging accompanying this stage;
- Pro-environmental services taking into account environmental requirements and ensuring that the useful life of equipment is maximised;
- Reverse logistics – the flow of end-of-life products and packaging to the place of recovery or final disposal.

Creating and improving green supply chains is inextricably linked to assessing their management and environmental performance. Such tools include the following:

- Ecological supply chain analysis, which identifies and scores environmental impacts taking into account successive stages of the product life cycle.
- Analytical hierarchy process, which involves creating a model of the hierarchical structure of the decision-making process, calculating scores from the mutual comparison of criteria, testing the consistency of the preference matrix and classifying decision options.
- Modified strategic scorecard: introducing environmental indicators to evaluate four performance assessment perspectives (financial, customer, internal processes and development) (Ryszko, 2014).

## 2.3 Sustainability and sustainable marketing: definitions and practical examples

The attitudes, actions and processes in the economy mentioned above are making a sustainable approach to production and consumption increasingly popular. This is understood as sustainability and renewability and is identified with achieving not only economic but also environmental and social aims in the context of long-range balancing of intergenerational needs (Pabian, 2012). The expression 'sustainable development' was first used in the Brundtland Report compiled by the World Commission on Environment and Development (Lee & Carter, 2009, p. 97). It defined sustainable development as development that considers the needs of the present without compromising the ability of future generations to meet them. Subsequent authors add that sustainable development is about balancing the above-mentioned aims (Grudzewski et al., 2010, p. 303). According to Wang and Butkouskaya (2023), sustainability is the ability of an enterprise to nurture and support growth over time by effectively meeting the expectations of various stakeholders.

In the Polish market, the increase in importance of environmental issues is reflected in the fact that a definition of sustainable development ('social and economic development, in which there is a process of integrating political, economic and social activities, with preservation of the natural balance and sustainability of basic natural processes, in order to ensure the ability to meet the basic needs of individual communities or citizens of both the present and future generations') has been included in Article 5 of the Constitution of the Republic of Poland (Konstytucja Rzeczypospolitej polskiej, 1997). The definition clearly emphasises that pursuing sustainable development is the responsibility of the government, the business community and various communities, organisations and individual citizens, which is also highlighted by other authors (Boztepe, 2013). Sustainability is treated as a corporate philosophy rather than an ongoing strategy at the operational and functional level (Rudawska, 2019).

A natural consequence of the spread of the concept of sustainability is penetration of sustainable ideas into marketing, which should look at the process of satisfying the needs of market participants from a long-term perspective taking into account the well-being of future generations. In characterising the concept of marketing flowing from sustainable development, the terms 'sustainable', 'sustainable marketing', 'self-sustainable marketing' and 'sustainability marketing' also appear (Pabian, 2012). Sustainable marketing activity is understood to include a balanced study of the marketing environment, a balanced selection of target markets and a balanced set of marketing instruments. It also aims to educate and raise consumers' environmental awareness by promoting the pro-environmental parameters of proposed solutions (Boztepe, 2013). Sustainable behaviour is expected and announced in the market. This is understood as a set of practical, deliberate and pre-emptive practices supporting the preservation of natural resources, including the standards of animal and plant life, and the social welfare of all generations (Nguyen & Mogaji, 2022, p. 253).

A sustainable consumer is one who strives to make his or her consumption sustainable, that is, one who is economically, environmentally and socially responsible (Zaremba-Warnke, 2016).

Sustainable marketing is the natural next stage in the evolution of marketing. In the evolution of conventional marketing, relationship marketing emerged, emphasising relationships instead of the earlier focus on the execution of transactions. A further development of marketing is social marketing and environmental marketing, that is, including social and environmental elements among the factors influencing marketing. Sustainable marketing is a synthesis of the trends mentioned above and can be defined as the process of satisfying the needs of consumers and society by planning and realising the concepts of benefits, costs, communication and convenience associated with the product offered in a way that satisfies the parties to the exchange and at the same time complies with the principles of sustainable development (Zaremba-Warnke, 2015). Satisfying needs following the principles of sustainable development requires recognition of the primacy of collective long-term needs related to sustainable development over the individual short-term needs of the parties to the exchange. Both parties – the offeror and the recipient – should recognise the sustainable development goals as priority framework conditions for satisfying all other needs. In this perspective, the natural environment is also a party to the exchange, since every exchange process has a greater or lesser impact on the environment, from which substances are taken and into which substances are discharged.

This trend entails changing the behaviour of virtually all the actors in a value chain, including producers and consumers. Today, the need to reconcile the continued focus of material marketing on stimulating consumption with a more sustainable use of natural resources is becoming very important. Companies' primary aim of maximising customer satisfaction is being replaced by gradually maximising sustainable consumption (Rudawska, 2013). This means that companies are pursuing aims centred around the environmental, social and economic areas (Palić & Bedek, 2010, pp. 1443–1456). The consequence is ensuring environmental, social (equity) and financial (economic) sustainability. These three elements are referred to in the literature as the 3Es (Hunt, 2011).

At the core of sustainable marketing development is the relationship between man and nature. In this relationship, it is man who is more dependent on nature's goods and its condition (Löbler, 2017). Therefore, for some authors (e.g., Jung et al., 2020), sustainable marketing is a process in which an enterprise needs to meet consumer demands, work hard at sustainable development (including ecology, economy and society in the entire production and operation) and build a long-term relationship with consumers.

A broader view of sustainable marketing is presented by Rudawska (2019), who defines it as the process of planning, organising and implementing marketing programmes related to the development of products, prices, sales methods and promotions in such a way as to satisfy customers and meet their needs, enable the company to achieve its goals and ensure that these processes are compatible with the ecosystem.

As a result of many market factors, new megatrends in consumption are emerging. The most relevant to the development of sustainable marketing are conscientious consumption, eco-consumption, deconsumption, prosumption, smart shopping and domocentrism. These megatrends in everyday life are manifested in the following behaviours and attitudes:

- Considering the social, economic and political consequences before making purchases. The immediate result will be the development of a sharing economy and an increased interest in exchanging. This will be complemented by retro-consumption, that is, referring to old recipes and technologies when shopping and satisfying needs, and following individuality and uniqueness. Within this group of behaviours, strictly anti-consumption behaviours are also emerging, as is exemplified by freeganism, which involves meeting food needs using products from restaurant surplus withdrawn from sale and even trash. It is so popular that it can rely on the support of various apps (e.g., Too Good To Go, https://www.toogoodtogo.com)

to find places where such products can be obtained for free or at a steep discount.

- The 3R rule, or reduce, reuse and recycle, is becoming commonplace. Based on this slogan, consumers are increasingly conscientiously reducing their consumption and do not need to keep buying newer and newer models. The causes of deconsumption can be categorised into four main groups: reducing consumption for rational reasons; reducing consumption due to an increase in the uncertainty of the situation of households (pandemic, wars and other sources of economic instability and the resulting uncertainty); reducing the number of goods consumed in favour of quality; and reducing consumption in the material sphere in favour of the servitisation of consumption (Woś, 2003).
- Devoting time and an organisational commitment to seeking offers that are most attractively priced. This is associated with a low level of loyalty to existing providers of goods and an increase in the efficiency of searches for price promotions and alternative ways of satisfying needs. Consumers analyse not only the price parameters of products but also their composition and country of origin, and the image of the product provider. The development of digital technology makes it possible for them to do this on an essentially continual basis and quickly make a selection of the most attractive offers.
- An important area of consumer functioning is becoming their home space, in which they primarily develop their family life. There is a phenomenon of privatisation of consumption, that is, replacing public consumption with private consumption. In this way, consumers seek to satisfy nutritional, cultural, educational and social needs. The domocentralisation of consumption contributes to consumers focusing on their own homes and immediate family and a kind of celebration of domesticity.
- Greater consumer awareness also means an increase in the popularity of prosumer attitudes (Vergura et al., 2023). Consumers are aware of their power to influence their relationships with producers. They are getting involved in commenting, evaluating and making suggestions for change. Manufacturers also increasingly value this involvement and information coming from the market (ElShafei, 2022). Market research is becoming the basis for developing offerings and creating new market solutions (Yıldırım, 2021). As a result, the conscientious, pro-environmental and solidarity attitudes increasingly manifested by buyers in the decision-making process, in the light of eco-consumption, conscientious consumption and prosumption, can be catalysts for positive changes in the process of creating innovative food products, precisely thanks to green marketing initiatives taken (Kozłowski & Rutkowska, 2018).

The ambiguity and high capacity of sustainability and sustainable marketing concepts mean that they are treated as signposts rather than precise strategies

(Salciuviene et al., 2022). However, to operationalise these concepts, there is a need to define criteria for a company to assess the sustainability of products and processes. These can be divided into three groups (Zaremba-Warnke, 2015): ecological, economic and socio-cultural. Ecological criteria include the following:

- not harming the climate;
- not harming the natural landscape;
- not harming nature and biodiversity;
- using non-renewable resources;
- no health risks.

Among the economic factors can be distinguished as follows:

- economic effects;
- satisfaction of needs at the rational price level;
- inflationary effects and effects on capital concentration;
- dependence on the supply of raw materials (such as the intensity of transport);
- technical efficiency and competition for access to resources.

The main socio-cultural factors are as follows:

- concern for security, quality of life and health;
- conflict avoidance;
- integration in existing structures;
- poverty eradication and sustainable security of supply;
- participatory democracy and social acceptability.

## 2.4 Adverse consumer trends slowing the development of sustainable marketing

It would not only be incomplete but also unfair to present the history of the development of sustainable marketing without showing trends contrary to the ideas that are simultaneously developing worldwide. Hedonism among part of the public combined with the environmental ignorance of an equally large group of consumers makes these environmentally unfavourable trends popular. Fast fashion and consumerism intensifying compulsive and impulsive purchasing have been identified as the most visible and negative influences on sustainable attitudes, trends and phenomena (Japutra et al., 2018).

One of the most important trends, which is a source of a large amount of waste and environmental pollution, is fast fashion (Mróz-Gorgoń, 2015), a new sales model in the clothing industry characterised by the instantaneous use of developing trends in new models of clothes and accessories on sale (Liu et al., 2021). In this trend, the final result of efforts by manufacturers is heavily promoted and inexpensive clothing products (Sanchez et al., 2017). With a very dynamic approach to trend-tracking, the concept of the season almost ceases to apply, and the determinant becomes the number of clothing items introduced for sale during the year (Sempruch-Krzemińska, 2014; Sempruch-Krzemińska et al., 2016). Collections used to be released four times a year. Today, many brands are already talking about 52 'micro-collections' a year. Some well-known chain stores even release 500 designs a week (Environmental Audit Committee, 2019). Thanks to global supply chains and flexibility in designing and manufacturing these products, bidders can quickly react to new trends and demands in different places on Earth and at other times. It gives them a decisive competitive advantage over traditional clothing manufacturers. It makes their products cheap and very attractive to consumers (McCormick & Livett, 2012). This fact makes the trend particularly dangerous for the environment. More and more often, information emerges in the media about significant batches of unsold clothing that end up in the rubbish waiting for someone to dispose of them. Fast fashion products are so cheap that it is unprofitable for some brands to offer returns from misplaced purchases for resale. The costs of disinfecting, ironing and repackaging are too high, exceeding the price of products. Returned and full-priced products go straight into the rubbish.

When low price is the priority, the consequence is low-quality materials being used to produce clothes which are increasingly difficult to recycle. Quite often unsold and/or damaged products in the fast fashion sector are incinerated. A system of collecting used clothing from the public was seen as a partial solution to the problem (Mohammad et al., 2020). Poland still has a network of containers for used clothing (in addition, from time to time some charitable organisations organise collections of clothes for people in need). Nevertheless, there are so many used clothes that organisations dealing with them cannot keep up with managing them, and more piles of rubbish are created. Examples of challenges facing the fashion industry today include the following:

- 22 million tons of textile waste are discarded each year in the United States. That is about 2,150 garments a second;
- 87% of the cloth used to make clothing is ultimately incinerated or sent to landfill;
- according to research, on average people wear a piece of clothing only ten times before throwing it away (Deloitte, 2023).

Some measures can be taken to reduce the consumption of clothing in the modern world. Some companies deliberately make clothes and accessories (such as the Patagonia brand) in their collections to be more eco-friendly.

However, on the other hand, they still encourage people to buy more clothes (Sung & Jeon, 2009). Recycled materials are also becoming fashionable, and clothing manufacturers are increasingly including them in the composition of their clothes. But this is still only a fragment of the business. Standard practices that do not take into account pro-environmental standards still prevail. One can sometimes get the impression that the willingness of ordinary citizens to engage in sustainable shopping is shattered by an inability to organise these practices systematically.

Oversupply of various products (not only clothing) and difficulty in selling them cause manufacturers to intensify promotional and sales activities to convince customers to make more purchases. Unfortunately, the fight for sales in an enterprise often wins out over concern for the environment. In this endeavour, entrepreneurs take advantage of further advances in psychological knowledge, making it increasingly common for individual purchases to become impulsive or even compulsive. Increasingly effective sales techniques are causing consumers to buy more random unnecessary products. Fast fashion offerings include cheap products, short product runs and low quality. These factors determine frequent purchases. Impulse buying is a consumer response to product features, and it is driven by a (real or imagined) need for the product itself. The impulse can be a factor in the consumer's environment regarding the decor of the shop or product, such as an attractive display arrangement, a pleasant smell in the showroom, an attractive product price, a favourable appearance, an aesthetically pleasing way of displaying the offer, a reasonable opinion of the salesperson or pleasant service in the shop (Rahman & Mannan, 2018). Customers who treat consumption as a source of pleasant stimuli are more likely to have an emotional approach to shopping and are more likely to make impulsive purchases. However, impulsive shopping is not synonymous with irrational shopping. Indeed, it often happens that a customer is much more satisfied with a previously unplanned purchase than one undertaken after a meticulous comparison of offers. Usually, a rational decision-making process occurs during such purchases, but it is carried out much faster and occurs at the point of sale.

Compulsive shopping, conversely, results primarily from a sheer need to buy underpinned by the consumer's emotional or mental problems. Compulsive buying is chronic repetitive buying that mainly responds to an individual's adverse events and feelings. Among the factors that initiate compulsive shopping are low self-esteem, lack of self-acceptance, stress, low mood, a desire to unwind and negative emotions. The purpose of such purchasing is to temporarily improve one's mood. However, often after a purchase the customer reacts negatively, usually with anger and shame. As a result, the consumer purchases a product he does not need, does not want or does not like. This leads to renewed deterioration of the customer's mental state. This cycle, in extreme cases, drives vulnerable customers into addiction – shopaholism (Nallaperuma et al., 2022).

## 2.5 Planned product obsolescence

Trends that run counter to sustainability include the phenomenon of planned product obsolescence, which is defined as prompting consumers of durable goods to replace them with new ones, even though the old ones are still usable (Proszowska, 2013). According to another source (Ryś, 2017), planned product obsolescence is deliberately designing products to be suitable for replacement with a newer model after a short period. Planned obsolescence is also defined as stimulating consumer demand by creating products that wear out or become obsolete after a limited period (Proszowska, 2014). Other terms for manipulation of this kind are 'creative destruction', 'progressive age adjustment', 'quality reduction', 'death dating' and determining 'product shelf life' (Proszowska, 2013). A companion term to planned obsolescence is the concept of anti-features, or ways to make household appliances function below their factory capacity (Prucnel, 2012). Some sources (Rivera & Lallmahomed, 2016) also distinguish between types of planned obsolescence, which are as follows:

- obsolescence of function – a product breaks down or otherwise becomes unusable in an extremely short period;
- obsolescence of style – seen, for example, in the clothing industry, in which successive collections radically depreciate those of the previous season;
- technical obsolescence – an old product is pushed out of the market by a new one with similar functions.

This phenomenon can also be observed in the world of textbooks, successive editions of which for learning the same curricular content differ from each other so significantly that they force consecutive generations of pupils and students to buy new books instead of the cheaper used editions of previous years (Proszowska, 2014). In this way, books that could serve for many years are discarded after one use.

Some products are designed to ensure cyclical consumption, enabling the economy to grow. At the same time, this results in the production of endless toxic waste (or at best unnecessary waste paper) and poses a threat to life on Earth (Ryś & Prymon-Ryś, 2017). Planned obsolescence causes people to buy certain products more often than they should, making them unable to afford all their needs and producing more rubbish than they should (Rivera & Lallmahomed, 2016).

Planned product obsolescence contradicts the ideas of sustainability and corporate social responsibility, and despite some initial benefits of its use (stimulating economic development through increased consumption), it leads the world to decline instead of helping realise dreams of spectacular development (Zuboff, 2019).

The drive to make as much profit as possible is a powerful incentive to act. Certainly, planned product obsolescence cannot be completely eliminated from the modern economy. However, it is already negatively perceived by consumers (especially in situations where it threatens consumers' lives or health, such as in some sectors of the medical industry), and companies using it are facing increasing social ostracism.

According to many studies (e.g., Prucnel, 2012), it is often cheaper to re-use a product than to recycle an old one and use a new one. Therefore, for example, putting a computer in working order consumes about 20 times less energy than producing a new one. This is why many organisations (such as the Dutch Platform 21 Foundation) are beginning to encourage users to repair old equipment. At the same time, they are calling on manufacturers to include instructions in equipment manuals on how to improve products themselves. At IEEE (American Institute of Electrical and Electronics Engineers) conferences, examples are presented of products that can be taken apart, repaired and made ready for use again after manufacture.

In addition to this, in an era of massively increasing access to information and increasing difficulty for companies to control knowledge, it should be assumed that it will become more accessible and easier to find out how a product is made and to choose one that has the needs of consumers in mind first and foremost (Naderer & Opree, 2021). There will be telephone and computer programmes and applications that allow customers to assess the actual cost of using a given solution, considering the useful life of a given offering. Already today, one of the elements differentiating offerings is the repairability (i.e., the ability of users to repair a product without spending significant amounts of time and resources, Kotler & Keller, 2012, p. 354) of goods and services, with companies offering technical support via fax, telephone or the internet for self-repair of purchased equipment.

Planned product obsolescence is only possible when there is information asymmetry with the customer only having the knowledge provided by manufacturers (Proszowska, 2013). An informed consumer must learn to seek, evaluate and select information. Today's marketplace is also increasingly becoming a forum for co-creation experiences, where there is a dialogue between consumers (or even prosumers) and the producer to co-create value (Rupik, 2012, p. 218). It is hoped that the prevalence of this phenomenon will also reduce planned product ageing.

## 2.6 Greenwashing

Since consumers value pro-environmental aspects of companies' practices, it is evident that they are tempted to emphasise these aspects of their market activity in their communication with the market (Orea-Giner & Fusté-Forné, 2023). It is difficult to begrudge businesses for this. It is worse when sustainability practices are not the result of a consistently implemented sustainable strategy and part of a continual improvement process in this area but minor episodes calculated to impress the public. This phenomenon is called 'greenwashing'. The term was coined by New York environmentalist Jay Westervelt in 1980 (Braga Junior et al., 2019; Romero, 2008); however, it came into common use after 1996 (Greer & Bruno, 1996). Today, the literature (Budzanowska-Drzewiecka & Proszowska, 2023) distinguishes the following two different approaches to defining the concept:

- greenwashing is decoupling behaviour, an action designed to divert attention from a company's non-environmental activities (Walker & Wan, 2012) and
- greenwashing is selective disclosure associated with exposing pro-environmental practices as elements sought by the message's audience (Delmas & Burbano, 2011; Tateishi, 2018).

Greenwashing as a marketing tool has developed intensively and can take many forms in the activities of enterprises. Distinctions include (Willis et al., 2023) greencrowding, greenhushing, greenlabelling, greenlighting, greenrising and greenshifting. All these are varieties of intensive exposure of individual pro-environmental initiatives of companies while hiding environmentally harmful activities, reducing the actual negative impact and shifting responsibility for the state of the environment to consumers. Organised massive misleading of consumers and other stakeholders is facilitated by a lack of uniform standards for reporting corporate socially responsible activities. It is difficult for recipients of information to assess the real significance of an initiative and its impact on the environment.

Customers perceive consciously identified greenwashing very negatively (Braga Junior et al., 2019; Jog & Singhal, 2019). However, on a day-to-day basis, consumers find it challenging to identify activities of this kind (Lee et al., 2016; Wang et al., 2020). Identifying greenwashing is possible when the buyer has extensive knowledge of the company and its operations and specialised knowledge of the technology used and the alternatives to this way of satisfying needs (Akturan, 2018). For more expensive durable goods, the customers may prepare themselves in this way for the transaction they are entering into. However, it will be completely different, for example, for small products bought on impulse. Then, the knowledge of the offer is incomplete and it is impossible to fully evaluate the company's policy. Various types of ranking and certification are helpful for customers. They lend credibility to the practices of entities that have such documents and make it easier to assess how sustainable a company's policies are.

For this reason, environmental certificates are very popular among entrepreneurs. They are an essential attribute of companies that identify themselves as environmentally conscious. The only problem is that these certifications are too diverse and fragmented, making it sometimes difficult to appreciate the importance of the most prestigious and significant ones when it comes to environmental issues (Kumar et al., 2021).

A major complication when assessing the real significance of greenwashing in the development of sustainable marketing is the fact that individual activities are often not illegal but very confusing for consumers. Very often, a charitable nature of activities and a large scale of the venture effectively distract stakeholders from a harmful environmental impact of an enterprise's core business. This phenomenon is so strongly present in the promotion of culture and sport that the terms greenwashing culture (Miller, 2018) and greenwashing sport (Miller, 2017) have already appeared in the literature. They refer to policies such as sponsorship of cultural and sporting initiatives (competitions, festivals, entire sports teams, individual athletes, artists, etc.) by companies with significantly negative environmental impacts (e.g., gas and petroleum companies).

## 2.7 Trends supporting the development of sustainable attitudes

Noting the detrimental impact on the environment of the negative trends in consumer behaviour mentioned above (and other ones), some social groups and organisations are trying to popularise attitudes and actions that can stop or at least reduce these damaging processes (Byrd & Su, 2021). For example, it is possible, among other things, with educational programmes in the traditional education system (kindergartens, schools and universities) and training courses and workshops prepared by social organisations, businesses and individuals (Dardanoni & Guerriero, 2021). Quite often, these programmes aim to educate customers and service recipients in order to improve the operation of a business itself (e.g., waste segregation training organised by waste collection and recycling companies). Another reason for education activity in the field of sustainable consumption can be to draw attention to the sustainability parameters in a company's offer. Presenting the characteristics of sustainable manufacturing processes and how the raw materials for this production are obtained encourages consumers to analyse these processes in other providers of these products.

The list of trends that constitute the development of sustainable marketing at the beginning of this chapter can be supplemented with such terms as slow food, slow fashion, slow journeys and simply slow life. Slow life is a philosophy that began with a boycott of a fast food restaurant that, with a focus on speed and a low price, offered consumers low-quality meals. Today's followers of the slow movement celebrate simple natural ingredients of meals, preferably self-prepared, and satisfy their needs in a way that is as close to nature as possible. Organic foods and bioproducts which do not contain preservatives are becoming increasingly sought after (Oke et al., 2020; Wojciechowska-Solis & Soroka, 2017). Consumers are forced to buy conscientiously to avoid throwing away products that spoil faster. The disadvantage of these solutions is that they are much more expensive than 'fast' offerings. At the same time, the growing popularity of these solutions means they are slowly becoming cheaper (Amatulli et al., 2021).

Modern technology is also vital in developing sustainable consumption in the fashion sector. More products are designed using 3D design and sampling, so there are no physical prototypes of products, no wasted materials and no shipping costs. At the same time, it is possible to respond faster to market trends and consumer expectations (Jain et al., 2021). Printed models make it possible to assess the feasibility of projects. There is no need to take photos of a collection as its design is already digital. The whole process is less harmful to the environment. Clothing manufacturers use algorithms to track the movement of clothes along the production and supply chain, allowing them to predict demand and thus reduce product transport, for example. Artificial reality allows products to be tried on that have not yet been physically created, just their digital visualisation. Studies show that virtual fitting rooms contribute to a 27% reduction in the rate of returns resulting mainly from size mismatches or the wrong cut of a product. Wholesalers increasingly use virtual showrooms to help customers evaluate products and make better purchasing decisions without making additional trips or shipping prototypes.

A study by Deloitte (2023) clearly shows a substantial increase in consumer interest in sustainable fashion in Poland. On average, more than two in five consumers seek to only buy committed socially responsible brands caring for the environment. A total of 64% of consumers say they would pay more for products and services from brands committed to making a positive social impact. The offers of clothing manufacturers already increasingly include the possibility of returning used clothes, which later go into second-hand circulation (the 'Wear_Fair' programme in the 4F Charge project), and of renting luxury clothes and handbags (e.g., online rentals: https://e-garderobe.com/pl or https://www.fancyrent.pl/).

There are, of course, more of these types of innovations in all kinds of industries, and their growing number is undoubtedly a cause for optimism. However, the current situation causes some grumbling among responsible conscientious consumers when they realise how small sustainable marketing is. Recycling in the clothing industry means that globally 1% of garments are recycled into new clothes.

Pressure on the clothing industry to motivate the commitment of the fashion industry to sustainable transformation is not only from consumers. More regulations are emerging that are setting the stage for change in the industry. Significant catalysts for change include the following:

- the International Accord for Health and Safety in the Textile and Garment Industry – 2013;
- the European Green Deal – 2019;

- the Action Plan for a Circular Economy – 2020;
- the Sustainable and Circular Textile Strategy – 2020;
- the Proposed Eco-design for Sustainable Products Regulation – 2022;
- Adoption of the Corporate Sustainability Reporting Directive – 2022;
- the Draft Green Claims Directive – 2023;
- the Extended Producer Responsibility Proposal (Deloitte, 2023).

All indications are that we are at a point in which brands need to find an area where they will reliably change and communicate this responsibly and clearly. The next generations entering the market are showing an increasing sensitivity to sustainable practices by brands, and it is hoped that the response of businesses will be an increase in sustainable marketing, in its pure form without the taint of greenwashing.

However, it is important to bear in mind that sustainable consumption and production require a systematic approach and cooperation between actors along the supply chain, from producers to consumers. This process involves educational and other practices for consumers to raise their awareness of sustainable consumption and related lifestyles through, among other things, information campaigns on product standards and labelling.

In the initial stage, however, these practices are very complex and costly and cannot be sustained by individual companies. However, such measures also make economic sense because in the long term, sustainable consumption and production seek to do more and better with fewer resources. This leads to an increase in the net benefits of economic activity by reducing the consumption of materials and reducing the scale of degradation and pollution while improving the quality of life. This affects everyone – businesses, consumers, policymakers, researchers, scientists, retailers, the media, development cooperation organisations and others.

## References

Akturan, U. (2018). How does greenwashing affect green branding equity and purchase intention? An empirical research. *Marketing Intelligence and Planning*, *36*(7), 809–824. https://doi.org/10.1108/MIP-12-2017-0339

Amatulli, C., De Angelis, M., Pino, G., & Jain, S. (2021). Consumer reactions to unsustainable luxury: A cross-country analysis. *International Marketing Review*, *38*(2), 412–452. https://doi.org/10.1108/IMR-05-2019-0126

Białoń, L. (1998). Ekomarketing. In B. Poskrobko (Ed.), *Sterowanie ekorozwojem* (p. 121). Białystok: Wydawnictwo Politechniki Białostockiej.

Boztepe, A. (2013). Green marketing and its impact on consumer buying behavior. *International Journal of Engineering Science Invention*, European Journal of Economic and Political Studies, *2*(12), 61–64.

Braga Junior, S., Martínez, M. P., Correa, C. M., Moura-Leite, R. C., & Da Silva, D. (2019). Greenwashing effect, attitudes, and beliefs in green consumption. *RAUSP Management Journal*, *54*(2), 226–241. https://doi.org/10.1108/RAUSP-08-2018-0070

Brandys, J. (2013). Marketing ekologiczny – założenia, perspektywy. *Zeszyty Naukowe Wyższej Szkoły Zarządzania i Bankowości w Krakowie*, *27*, 53–65.

Bronakowski, H. (1997). *Rynek – marketing dóbr i usług ekologicznych (Słownik podstawowych pojęć)*. Białystok: Wydawnictwo Wyższej Szkoły Finansów i Zarządzania.

Bruhn, M., & Schnebelen, S. (2017). Integrated marketing communication – From an instrumental to a customer-centric perspective. *European Journal of Marketing*, *51*(3), 464–489. https://doi.org/10.1108/EJM-08-2015-0591

Budzanowska-Drzewiecka, M., & Proszowska, A. (2023). Greenwashing Knowledge as a Determinant of Consumer Engagement in Greenwashed Word of Mouth. *23rd International Joint Conference Central and Eastern Europe in the Changing Business Environment*, 25–39. https://doi.org/10.18267/pr.2023.kre.2490.2

Byrd, K., & Su, J. (2021). Investigating consumer behaviour for environmental, sustainable and social apparel. *International Journal of Clothing Science and Technology*, *33*(3), 336–352. https://doi.org/10.1108/IJCST-03-2020-0040

Constitutional Court. (1997).

Corrado, L., Fazio, A., & Pelloni, A. (2021). Pro-environmental attitudes, local environmental conditions and recycling behavior. *CEIS* Working Paper No. 513, *19*(4), 1–37.

Dardanoni, V., & Guerriero, C. (2021). Young people's willingness to pay for environmental protection. *Ecological Economics*, *179*(March 2020), 106853. https://doi.org/10.1016/j.ecolecon.2020.106853

Delmas, M. A., & Burbano, V. C. (2011). The drivers of greenwashing. *California Management Review*, *54*(1), 64–87. https://doi.org/10.1525/cmr.2011.54.1.64

Deloitte. (2023). *Brand Purpose. Rynek mody.* https://www2.deloitte.com/pl/pl/services/deloitte-digital/Raport-Brand-Purpose-rynek-mody.html

ElShafei, R. (2022). Managers' risk perception and the adoption of sustainable consumption strategies in the hospitality sector: The moderating role of stakeholder salience attributes. *Smart and Sustainable Built Environment*, *11*(1), 1–18. https://doi.org/10.1108/SASBE-03-2020-0024

Finne, Å, & Grönroos, C. (2017). Communication-in-use: Customer-integrated marketing communication. *European Journal of Marketing*, *51*(3), 445–463.

Greer, J., & Bruno, K. (1996). *Greenwash: The Reality Behind Corporate Environmentalism*. Rowman & Littlefield Publishers.

Gregor, B., & Kalicińska-Kula, M. (2014). *Badania marketingowe na użytek decyzji menedżerskich*. Łódź: Wydawnictwo Uniwersytetu Łódzkiego.

Grudzewski, W., Hejduk, I., Sankowska, A., & Wańtuchowicz, M. (2010). *Sustainability w biznesie, czyli przedsiębiorstwo przyszłości. Zmiany paradygmatów i koncepcji zarządzania*. Warszawa: Poltext.

Hansen, F. (1973). Psychological theories of consumer choice. *Journal of Consumer Research*, *3*, 117–142.

Hervani, A. A., Helms, M. M., & Sarkis, J. (2005). Performance measurement for green supply chain management. *Benchmarking: An International Journal*, *12*(4), 330–353.

Honkanen, P., & Young, J. A. (2015). What determines British consumers 'motivation to buy sustainable seafood'? *British Food Journal*, *117*(4), 1289–1302. https://doi.org/10.1108/BFJ-06-2014-0199

Hunt, S. (2011). Sustainable marketing, equity, and economic growth: A resource-advantage, economic freedom approach. *Journal of the Academy of Marketing Science*, *39*(1). https://e-garderobe.com/pl; https://www.fancyrent.pl.

Inieke, O. (2021). Sustainable development goals, are we there yet?–Challenges and shortcomings. *World Journal of Science, Technology and Sustainable Development*, *18*(3), 320–324. https://doi.org/10.1108/wjstsd-06-2020-0053

Jain, G., Paul, J., & Shrivastava, A. (2021). Hyper-personalization, co-creation, digital clienteling and transformation. *Journal of Business Research*, *124*(June), 12–23. https://doi.org/10.1016/j.jbusres.2020.11.034

Jaiswal, D., Singh, B., Kant, R., & Biswas, A. (2022). Towards green product consumption: Effect of green marketing stimuli and perceived environmental knowledge in Indian consumer market. *Society and Business Review*, *17*(1), 45–65. https://doi.org/10.1108/SBR-05-2021-0081

Japutra, A., Ekinci, Y., Simkin, L., & Nguyen, B. (2018). The role of ideal self-congruence and brand attachment in consumers 'negative behaviour. Compulsive buying and external trash-talking. *European Journal of Marketing*, *52*(3/4), 683–701. https://doi.org/10.1108/EJM-06-2016-0318

Jog, D., & Singhal, D. (2019). Pseudo green players and their greenwashing practices: A differentiating strategy for real green firms of personal care category. *Strategic Direction*, *35*(12), 4–7. https://doi.org/10.1108/SD-07-2019-0143

Jung, J., Kim, S. J., & Kim, K. H. (2020). Sustainable marketing activities of traditional fashion market and brand loyalty. *Journal of Business Research*, *120*, 294–301. https://doi.org/10.1016/j.jbusres.2020.04.019

Kamiński, J. (2019). Zrównoważony marketing w zrównoważonym świecie — Cz. 2. *Marketing i Rynek*, *3*, 5–16.

Karjaluoto, H., Mustonen, N., & Ulkuniemi, P. (2015). The role of digital channels in industrial marketing communications. *Journal of Business and Industrial Marketing*, *30*(6), 703–710. https://doi.org/10.1108/JBIM-04-2013-0092

Khan, R., Awan, T. M., Fatima, T., & Javed, M. (2021). Driving forces of green consumption in sharing economy. *Management of Environmental Quality: An International Journal*, *32*(1), 41–63. https://doi.org/10.1108/MEQ-03-2020-0052

Kitchen, P. J., & Burgmann, I. (2015). Integrated marketing communication: Making it work at a strategic level. *The Journal of Business Strategy*, *36*(4), 34–39.

Kitchen, P. J., & Proctor, T. (2015). Marketing communications in a post-modern world. *Journal of Business Strategy*, *36*(5), 34–42. https://doi.org/10.1108/JBS-06-2014-0070

Konstytucja Rzeczypospolitej Polskiej z dnia 2 kwietnia 1997 r., Dz.U. 1997 no 78, is. 483.

Kotler, P., & Keller, K. L. (2012). *Marketing*. Warszawa: REBIS.

Kozielski, R. (2011). Ewolucja komunikacji rynkowej a model budowania sukcesu organizacji – aspekty strategiczne, operacyjne, organizacyjne i finansowe. In B. Pilarczyk (Ed.), *Komiunikacja rynkowa. Strategie i instrumenty*, 42–52. Poznań: Uniwersytet Ekonomiczny w Poznaniu.

Kozłowski, W., & Rutkowska, A. (2018). Megatrendy w konsumpcji żywności a marketing społecznie zaangażowany Streszczenie. *Handel Wewnętrzny*, *2*(373), 261–269.

Kumar, P., Polonsky, M., Dwivedi, Y. K., & Kar, A. (2021). Green information quality and green brand evaluation: The moderating effects of eco-label credibility and consumer knowledge. *European Journal of Marketing*, *55*(7), 2037–2071. https://doi.org/10.1108/EJM-10-2019-0808

Kumar Kar, S., & Harichandan, S. (2022). Green marketing innovation and sustainable consumption: A bibliometric analysis. *Journal of Cleaner Production*, *361*, 132290. https://doi.org/10.1016/j.jclepro.2022.132290

Lee, H. R., Jai, T. M. C., & Li, X. (2016). Guests' perceptions of green hotel practices and management responses on TripAdvisor. *Journal of Hospitality and Tourism Technology*, *7*(2), 182–199. https://doi.org/10.1108/JHTT-10-2015-0038

Lee, K., & Carter, S. (2009). *Global Marketing Management*. Oxford: Oxford University Press.

Lisowski, R., Mamcarczyk, M., Proszowska, A., & Soler-Porta, M. (2022). Pro-environmental attitudes and behaviours of young adults in shaping the market offer in the international dimension. *International Entrepreneurship Review*, *8*(4), 57–69. http://dx.doi.org/10.15678/IER.2022.0804.04

Lisowski, R., Proszowska, A., & Woźniak, M. (2021). The use of electricity by young adults in Poland and their other pro-environmental behaviours – case study of the AGH Faculty of Management. *Innovation Management and Sustainable Economic Development in the Era of Global Pandemic (IBIMA)*, 5610–5620.

Liu, Y., Liu, M. T., Perez, A., Chan, W., Collado, J., & Mo, Z. (2021). The importance of knowledge and trust for ethical fashion consumption. *Asia Pacific Journal of Marketing and Logistics*, *33*(5), 1175–1194. https://doi.org/10.1108/APJML-02-2020-0081

Löbler, H. (2017). Humans' relationship to nature – Framing sustainable marketing. *Journal of Services Marketing*, *31*(1), 73–82. https://doi.org/10.1108/JSM-01-2016-0037

Marek, E., & Jerzyk, E. (2018). Libertariański paternalizm, zielony marketing i neuronauka jako filary zrównoważonego rozwoju. *Handel Wewnętrzny*, *4*(375), 200–209.

McCormick, H., & Livett, C. (2012). Analysing the influence of the presentation of fashion garments on young consumers' online behaviour. *Journal of Fashion Marketing and Management*, *16*(1), 21–41. https://doi.org/10.1108/13612021211203014

Miller, T. (2017). *Greenwashing Sport*. London: Routledge.

Miller, T. (2018). *Greenwashing Culture*. London: Routledge.

Mirońska, D. (2010). Zachowania nabywców na rynku – trendy i wpływ na działanie przedsiębiorstw. *International Journal of Management and Economics*, *27*, 114–132.

Mohammad, J., Quoquab, F., & Mohamed Sadom, N. Z. (2020). Mindful consumption of second-hand clothing: The role of eWOM, attitude and consumer engagement. *Journal of Fashion Marketing and Management*, *25*(3), 482–510. https://doi.org/10.1108/JFMM-05-2020-0080

Mróz-Gorgoń, B. (2015). Polskie marki modowe w świadomości młodych konsumentów. *Zeszyty Naukowe Wyższej Szkoły Bankowej We Wrocławiu*, *15*(3), 441–449. http://ojs.wsb.wroclaw.pl/index.php/WSBRJ/article/viewFile/149/108

Naderer, B., & Opree, S. J. (2021). Increasing advertising literacy to unveil disinformation in green advertising. *Environmental Communication*, *15*(7), 923–936. https://doi.org/10.1080/17524032.2021.1919171

Nagy, S., Piskóti, I., Molnár, L., & Marien, A. (2012). The relationship between values and general environmental behaviour. *Economics and Management*, *17*(1), 272–278.

Naisbitt, J. (1982). *Megatrends: Ten New Directions Transforming Our Lives*. New York: Warner Books.

Nallaperuma, K., Septianto, F., & Bandyopadhyay, A. (2022). Mixed emotional appeal enhances advertising effectiveness of pro-environmental luxury brands: The mediating role of cognitive flexibility. *Asia Pacific Journal of Marketing and Logistics*, *34*(1), 175–189. https://doi.org/10.1108/APJML-10-2020-0719

Nguyen, N. P., & Mogaji, E. (2022). A theoretical framework for the influence of green marketing communication on consumer behaviour in emerging economies. In E. Mogaji, O. Adeola, I. Adisa, R. E. Hinson, C. Mukonza & C. A. Kirgiz (Eds.), *Green Marketing in Emerging Economies, 253–274*, Palgrave Studies of Marketing in Emerging Economies, Palgrave Macmillan, London. https://doi.org/10.1007/978-3-030-82572-0_11

Oke, A., Ladas, J., & Bailey, M. (2020). Ethical consumers: An exploratory investigation of the ethical food consumption behaviour of young adults in the North East of Scotland. *British Food Journal*, *122*(11), 3623–3638. https://doi.org/10.1108/BFJ-10-2019-0801

Orea-Giner, A., & Fusté-Forné, F. (2023). The way we live, the way we travel: Generation Z and sustainable consumption in food tourism experiences. *British Food Journal*, *125*(13), 330–351. https://doi.org/10.1108/BFJ-11-2022-0962

Pabian, A. (2012). Zrównoważony marketing na rynku przedsiębiorstw. *Zeszyty Naukowe Uniwersytetu Ekonomicznego w Poznaniu*, *2012*(226), 125–133.

Palić, M., & Bedek, A. (2010). Application of sustainability marketing practice among Croatian top brands. In L. Galetic & M. M. I. Spremić (Eds.), *An Enterprise Odyssey: From Crisis to Prosperity – Challenges for Government and Business*. Ekonomski Fakultet ZaZagreb.

Peattie, K. (1995). *Environmental Marketing Management: Meeting the Green Challenge*. London: Pitman Publishing.

Powell, M., & Osborne, S. P. (2015). Can marketing contribute to sustainable social enterprise? *Social Enterprise Journal*, *11*(1), 24–46. https://doi.org/10.1108/sej-01-2014-0009

Priest, J., Statt, D. A., & Carter, S. (2013). *Consumer Behaviour* (Vol. 2013). Edinburgh: Edingurgh Business School Herriot-Watt University.

Proszowska, A. (2013). Planowane postarzanie produktów przez przedsiębiorstwa – ujęcie problemowe. *Handel Wewnętrzny*, *1*, 207–213.

Proszowska, A. (2014). Planned Product Obsolescence - Reasons for It's Success and Prospects for the Future. *Proceedings of the International Conference Marketing Trends, 24th-25th January 2014*. http://archives.marketing-trends-congress.com/2014/pages/PDF/301.pdf

Prucnel, M. (2012). *Antyfunkcje – im nowszy produkt, tym krócej służy?*

Rahman, M. S., & Mannan, M. (2018). Consumer online purchase behavior of local fashion clothing brands. Information adoption, e-WOM, online brand familiarity and online brand experience. *Journal of Fashion Marketing and Management*, *22*(3), 404–419. https://doi.org/10.1108/JFMM-11-2017-0118

Rivera, J. L., & Lallmahomed, A. (2016). Environmental implications of planned obsolescence and product lifetime: A literature review. *International Journal of Sustainable Engineering*, *9*(2), 119–129. https://doi.org/10.1080/19397038.2015.1099757

Romero, P. (2008). *Beware of Green Marketing, Warns Greenpeace exec. ABS-CBN*. www.abs-cbnnews.com/special-report/09/16/08/beware-green-marketing-warns-greenpeace-exec

Rudawska, E. (2013). Marketing Zrównoważony – Nowe Oblicze Kapitalizmu? *Sustainable Marketing – A New Face of Capitalism? 24*(3), 75–88. http://search.ebscohost.com/login.aspx?direct=true&db=bsh&AN=93288356&site=ehost-live

Rudawska, E. (2019). Sustainable marketing strategy in food and drink industry: A comparative analysis of B2B and B2C SMEs operating in Europe. *Journal of Business and Industrial Marketing, 34*(4), 875–890. https://doi.org/10.1108/JBIM-05-2018-0171

Rupik, K. (2012). Sfera i marketing innowacyjnych produktów odzieżowych. In L. Żabiński (Ed.), *Marketing produktów systemowych*. Warszawa: Polskie Wydawnictwo Ekonomiczne.

Ryś, A. (2017). Badanie percepcji zjawiska planowego postarzania produktów. *Marketing i Zarządzanie, 49*(3), 231–244.

Ryś, A., & Prymon-Ryś, E. (2017). Tworzenie wartości w przedsiębiorstwach produkcyjnych a zjawisko planowego postarzania produktu. *Handel Wewnętrzny, 1*, 327–335.

Ryszko, A. (2007). *Proaktywność przedsiębiorstw w zarządzaniu środowiskowym*. Gliwice: Wydawnictwo Politechniki Śląskiej.

Ryszko, A. (2014). Wybrane problemy zarządzania zielonym łańcuchem dostaw. *Logistyka, 5*, 2059–2066.

Salciuviene, L., Banytė, J., Vilkas, M., Dovalienė, A., & Gravelines, Ž (2022). Moral identity and engagement in sustainable consumption. *Journal of Consumer Marketing, 39*(5), 445–459. https://doi.org/10.1108/JCM-03-2021-4506

Sanchez, J. A., Francisco, T., & Arroyo, J. (2017). Building brand loyalty in e-commerce of fashion lingerie. *Journal of Fashion Marketing and Management, 21*(1), 103–114. http://dx.doi.org/10.1108/JFMM-05-2016-0047

Semprebon, E., Mantovani, D., Demczuk, R., Souto Maior, C., & Vilasanti, V. (2019). Green consumption: A network analysis in marketing. *Marketing Intelligence and Planning, 37*(1), 18–32. https://doi.org/10.1108/MIP-12-2017-0352

Sempruch-Krzemińska, K. (2014). Proces zakupu odzieży fast fashion. *Marketing i Rynek, 3*, 18–24.

Sempruch-Krzemińska, K., Kall, J., Perchla-Włosik, A., & Raciniewska, A. (2016). Zmiany w zachowaniach nabywców na rynku mody. *Studia i Prace WNEiZ, 43*(3), 371–380. https://doi.org/10.18276/sip.2016.44/2-01

Shang, K. C., Lu, C. S., & Li, S. (2010). A taxonomy of green supply chain management capability among electronics-related manufacturing firms in Taiwan. *Journal of Environmental Management, 91*(5), 1218–1226.

Sieńko, B. (2000). Ekomarketing jako instrument budowania strategii przedsiębiorstwa. *Prace Naukowe Akademii Ekonomicznej We Wrocławiu, 870*, 299–309.

Silva, M. E., Sousa-Filho, J. M., de, Yamim, A. P., & Diógenes, A. P. (2020). Exploring nuances of green skepticism in different economies. *Marketing Intelligence and Planning, 38*(4), 449–463. https://doi.org/10.1108/MIP-10-2018-0435

Siuda, P. (2012). *Kultury prosumpcji. O niemożności powstania globalnych i ponadpaństwowych społeczności fanów*. Instytut Dziennikarstwa Uniwersytetu Warszawskiego.

Sun, Y., Li, T., & Wang, S. (2022). "I buy green products for my benefits or yours": Understanding consumers' intention to purchase green products. *Asia Pacific Journal of Marketing and Logistics, 34*(8), 1721–1739. https://doi.org/10.1108/APJML-04-2021-0244

Sung, H., & Jeon, Y. (2009). A profile of Koreans: Who purchases fashion goods online? *Journal of Fashion Marketing and Management*, *13*(1), 79–97. https://doi.org/10.1108/13612020910939897

Taranko, T. (2015). *Komunikacja marketingowa. Istota, uwarunkowania, efekty*. Warszawa: Wolters Kluwer SA.

Tateishi, E. (2018). Craving gains and claiming "green" by cutting greens? An exploratory analysis of greenfield housing developments in Iskandar Malaysia. *Journal of Urban Affairs*, *40*(3), 370–393. https://doi.org/10.1080/07352166.2017.1355667

Thaler, R. H. (2009). *Nudge*. London: Penguin Publishing Group.

Vergura, D. T., Zerbini, C., Luceri, B., & Palladino, R. (2023). Investigating sustainable consumption behaviors: A bibliometric analysis. *British Food Journal*, *125*(13), 253–276. https://doi.org/10.1108/BFJ-06-2022-0491

Walker, K., & Wan, F. (2012). The harm of symbolic actions and green-washing: Corporate actions and communications on environmental performance and their financial implications. *Journal of Business Ethics*, *109*(2), 227–242. https://doi.org/10.1007/s10551-011-1122-4

Wanat, T. (2016). Wpływ ceny i asortymentu na częstość wizyt w sklepach typu fast fashion. In M. Sławińska (Ed.) *Handel we współczesnej gospodarce. Nowe wyzwania*, 271–282, Katedra Handlu i Marketingu Uniwersytetu Ekonomicznego w Poznaniu. http://www.wbc.poznan.pl/Content/388137/Handel.pdf

Wang, D., Walker, T., & Barabanov, S. (2020). A psychological approach to regaining consumer trust after greenwashing: The case of Chinese green consumers. *Journal of Consumer Marketing*, *37*(6), 593–603. https://doi.org/10.1108/JCM-06-2019-3257

Wang, J., & Butkouskaya, V. (2023). Sustainable marketing activities, event image, perceived value and tourists' behavioral intentions in the sports tourism. *Journal of Economics, Finance and Administrative Science*, *28*(55), 60–78. https://doi.org/10.1108/JEFAS-09-2022-0219

Wiktor, J. W. (2002). Modele komunikacji marketingowej. *Zeszyty Naukowe Akademii Ekonomicznej w Krakowie*, *602*, 115–124.

Willis, J., Bofiliou, T., Manili, A., Reynolds, I., & Kozlowski, N. (2023). The greenwashing hydra. In *Planet Tracker* (Issue January). https://*planet-tracker*.org/wp-content/uploads/2023/01/Greenwashing-Hydra-3.pdf

Wojciechowska-Solis, J., & Soroka, A. (2017). Motives and barriers of organic food demand among Polish consumers: A profile of the purchasers. *British Food Journal*, *119*(9), 2040–2048. https://doi.org/10.1108/BFJ-09-2016-0439

Woś, J. (2003). *Zachowania konsumenckie – teoria i praktyka*. Poznań: Wydawnictwo Akademii Ekonomicznej w Poznaniu.

Yıldırım, S. (2021). Do green women influencers spur sustainable consumption patterns? Descriptive evidences from social media influencers. *Ecofeminism and Climate Change*, *2*(4), 198–210. https://doi.org/10.1108/efcc-02-2021-0003

Zaremba-Warnke, S. (2000). Marketing ekologiczny. In G. Kobyłko (Ed.), *Proekologiczne zarządzanie przedsiębiorstwem*. Wrocław: Wydawnictwo Akademii Ekonomicznej we Wrocławiu.

Zaremba-Warnke, S. (2015). Marketing zrównoważony jako narzędzie doskonalenia przedsiębiorstwa. *Prace Naukowe Uniwersytetu Ekonomicznego We Wrocławiu*, *376*. https://doi.org/10.15611/pn.2015.376.07

Zavali, M., & Theodoropoulou, H. (2018). Investigating determinants of green consumption: Evidence from Greece. *Social Responsibility Journal*, *14*(4), 719–736. https://doi.org/10.1108/SRJ-03-2017-0042
Zawadzka, A. M. (2006). *Dlaczego przywiązujemy się do marki?* Gdańsk: Gdańskie Towarzystwo Psychologiczne.
Zuboff, S. (2019). *The Age of Surveillance Capitalism*. London: Profile books.

# 3 The main sustainable change actors

## 3.1 The concept of stakeholders

Originally, the term 'stakeholders' referred to an important group of people without which an organisation could not exist. By analysing the activities of the organisation, an effort was made to identify groups of external and internal factors that can give direction to the marketing activities of enterprises.

Since the end of the last century, as a response to the inadequacies of earlier strictly financial theories of business performance, a new conceptual model of business stakeholders (Freeman, 1984) has gained considerable acceptance. This model takes into account the environment of the organisation, legitimising new forms of activities in the organisation by focusing on their impact on the business environment (Wójcik-Karpacz, 2018). Models have been created that cluster impersonal and general macro-economy factors as in PESTEL analysis (PESTEL is an acronym for external factors affecting organisations: political, economic, social, technological, environmental and legal) (Song et al., 2017), while at the same time trying to identify sub-markets and partnerships crucial to the success of the organisation.

Starting in the 1970s, functional notions in stakeholder theory and related issues gradually evolved. A turning point occurred in 1984 when Freeman defined a stakeholder as 'any person or group that can influence or is influenced by the achievement of the organisation's objectives' (Freeman, 1984, p. 46). In the 1990s, researchers suggested a change and defined a stakeholder as 'a person who has influence on the organisation's achievement of its intended goals or a person who will be affected by the organisation's achievement of those goals (Baah et al., 2022). The focus was on defining the causality and subjectivity of the stakeholder. In addition, they pointed out the importance of the two-way relationship between the organisation and stakeholders. Bryson (1995, p. 27) proposed a more comprehensive definition: 'any person, group, or organisation that can place a claim on an organisation's attention, resources, or output or is affected by that output' (Freeman and Mcvea, 2001, p. 31). It is worth noting that according to project management manuals, stakeholders are individuals, groups and organisations that can influence the actions of an

DOI: 10.4324/9781003408642-4

individual or be influenced by the decisions made (Trocki et al., 2013). The Project Management Book of Knowledge, on the other hand, simplifies and practically frames stakeholders, including among them all persons, groups and organisations that are affected or influenced by a project, for example, customers, employees, cooperators, suppliers, business environment institutions, competitors, government and social institutions (PMBOK, 2021).

Stakeholder theory as developed in the previous century has the potential to be widely utilised in the implementation of the circular economy. This modern approach requires taking into account multiple perspectives, and all the entities involved in supporting sustainable changes must increasingly be guided not only by strictly environmental objectives but also by social, ethical and economic expectations in order to make changes that will not only have a long-term positive impact on the decisions of individuals and groups but will also be universally understood and accepted (Mirońska, 2016; Prymon-Ryś, 2015; Tait, 2020). The ability to identify key sustainable change actors and comprehend their motivations and capabilities is becoming increasingly important in implementing the circular economy idea in Poland.

## 3.2 Groups of stakeholders in a circular economy and a sustainable change

In the public debate on a circular economy, the dominant opinions often vary depending on the region, industry and specific issue being discussed. However, considering some common perspectives and modus operandi, the following interest groups may be identified as stakeholders of sustainable change (Lock & Seele, 2017). We can define a sustainable change as the process of making long-term sustainable improvements. This implies a transition toward a better system of human-environment relationships that remain within global limitations (Bitzer & Glasbergen, 2015).

*Environmental advocates*: environmental non-governmental organisations (NGOs) and individual activists frequently advocate a circular economy as a strategy to decrease waste, save resources and combat climate change. They work to raise awareness about green issues and are dedicated to supporting and disseminating practices that may protect the environment and its inhabitants (Jabbour et al., 2020). This group of stakeholders consists of not only members of NGOs but also volunteers, donors and sponsors. Economic think tanks should also be mentioned among this vast and diverse group of stakeholders. These groups are concerned with economic policy and may express views on how circular practices might affect economic growth, employment and resource management, and how the whole economy can benefit from sustainable development.

*International organisations*: not only NGOs but to a significant extent also transnational entities like the United Nations and the European Union have advocated and established goals related to a circular economy. Their opinions and initiatives influence global discussions and provide inspiration for lawmaking initiatives. With their resolutions, they legitimise the actions of many individual and organised environmental advocates.

*Government and other administrative institutions*: national governments are followers of the previously mentioned stakeholder groups, and at the same time, they are entities that can implement green strategies and play a crucial role in shaping the circular economy through regulations, incentives and policies. Their opinions can heavily influence the direction and pace of implementation of a circular economy on a national and regional scale (Jager & O'Riordan, 2019).

*Business and industry leaders*: since many business leaders and industry associations recognise the economic benefits of circular practices, such as cost savings, innovation opportunities, improved reputation and brand equity (Ishaq & Di Maria, 2020), they often promote circular economy principles to enhance their competitiveness. These stakeholders demonstrate their social and environmental responsibility and shape sustainable consumption patterns by launching green products, participating in pro-environmental initiatives and implementing sustainable production standards (Green Production Guide, 2016).

*Media and influencers*: the media and influential individuals, including celebrities and social media influencers, can shape the public debate and consumer perceptions and attitudes through widespread coverage, persuasive communication, commentary and environmental advocacy.

*Academics and researchers*: experts in fields related to sustainability and circular economics provide research-based insights and often advocate evidence-based decision-making. They provide scientific arguments for the need for sustainable change. Their impact on the education and learning of future generations should also be recognised.

*Consumers*: last but not least, public opinion is influenced by consumer attitudes and behaviours. Consumer preferences for green products and individual eco-friendly activities can impact company strategies and policymaking as consumer awareness of sustainability grows.

The impact of each of these stakeholder groups will be described more fully in subsections 3.4–3.8.

It is important to note that opinions on the circular economy can be diverse and complex, with various stakeholders advocating different aspects of sustainability and with different motivations. The balance between environmental, economic and social considerations in public debates can also vary. Ultimately, the dominant opinions in circular economy discourse may evolve as awareness and understanding of sustainability issues continue to grow. However, the idea of a circular economy has gained significant momentum and has been steadily acquiring more proponents, not only because of the urgency of environmental issues such as climate change, resource depletion and increasing environmental pollution but also because a growing number of consumers have become more environmentally conscious and prefer products and services that align with sustainability principles. This trend is supported by intense social awareness campaigns that highlight the benefits of a circular economy, thus contributing to positive perceptions of it and facilitating the implementation of policies and regulations that encourage circular economy practices.

Not everyone agrees with the principles of sustainability and a circular economy, and because stakeholders in sustainable change include not only proponents but also critics it is important to identify the primary causes of sustainable scepticism and rejection (Silva et al., 2020; Vergura et al., 2023; Wessels, 2013).

Some argue that sustainability measures can be costly to implement and may negatively impact economic growth, especially in industries which are heavily reliant on resource exploitation or environmentally harmful practices. They may resist sustainability measures due to concerns about profitability. This is because some businesses and individuals tend to prioritise short-term goals like immediate profits and convenience over long-term sustainability and broader societal and environmental concerns (Martinat et al., 2016).

Sustainability can be a politically divisive topic, with differing ideologies influencing people's views on the role of government in regulating and promoting it. Such cautious conservative behaviour by some politicians is connected with cultural norms and values, which can shape people's perspectives on sustainability, in particular with some cultures emphasising intense consumption as a sign of prosperity.

In terms of cultural values, 'resistance to sustainable change' should also be mentioned, as people often do not accept change (Lozano, 2009). This is especially true when adopting sustainable behaviour or practices requires significant changes in lifestyle or business operations. After all, not everyone is well-informed about sustainability issues. These people may question the validity of scientific evidence supporting them. Such lack of awareness and misconceptions about sustainability and its implications can lead to scepticism or opposition. Therefore, it is important to engage in constructive dialogue and address these concerns through education, research, policymaking and communication strategies. Building a consensus on the importance of sustainability often requires addressing diverse perspectives and finding common ground for action.

While there are still challenges, sceptics and barriers to widespread adoption, the overall trend has been towards greater support for a circular economy. The positive atmosphere around sustainability and circular practices has continued to grow, with more stakeholders recognising the importance of transitioning to a more sustainable circular model.

## 3.3 Consumers as benefactors and the main stakeholders in sustainable change

Circular marketing that focuses on promoting and communicating the principles and benefits of a circular economy involves approaches that emphasise sustainability, resource conservation and reduction of waste such as:

- engaging consumers in circular practices, such as encouraging repairing, recycling and responsibly disposing of products by loyalty programmes and incentives;
- providing educational content to raise awareness of the importance of a circular economy and how consumers can contribute;
- emphasising transparency by providing clear information about product materials, recycling options and sustainability efforts. This builds trust among environmentally conscious consumers. This approach is often supported by corporate social responsibility (CSR) efforts and reporting;
- highlighting circular practices by demonstrating how a company or product adheres to circular economy principles such as recycling, reusing and minimising waste in manufacturing and the supply chain. This includes sustainable packaging solutions such as using recycled materials, reducing packaging waste and designing packaging for easy recycling. In addition, this can involve 'product storytelling' to present the entire life cycle of a product from design and production to use, recycling and disposal to help consumers understand a product's environmental impact;
- collaborating and partnering with organisations and initiatives that promote sustainability and circular economy principles (Moser, 2016).

Circular marketing is a response to growing consumer demand for environmentally friendly and sustainable products. It aims to align marketing efforts with the values and expectations of consumers who prioritise sustainability and responsible consumption.

Individuals value a circular economy for a number of reasons. Environmentally conscious consumers see efficient use of depletable resources by reducing waste and extending the life of products as one of the key benefits of sustainable change. In addition, circular economy practices can lead to cost savings, job creation and economic growth by fostering innovation and new business models. As a result, they can improve product quality, affordability and access, benefiting consumers and reducing social inequalities.

These benefits are reinforced by many governments implementing policies and regulations that incentivise circular practices to address environmental challenges. In the context of public security, circular economy practices reduce dependence on scarce and geopolitically unstable resources, thereby enhancing the economic and resource security of nations. They offer a more sustainable and resilient way of operating in the face of global challenges such as climate change and resource scarcity.

Finally, society can recognise the overall environmental impact of production and consumption (i.e., reducing pollution and greenhouse gas emissions, adopting new lifestyles, etc.) as a benefit of sustainable change.

The drivers of consumer pro-environmental behaviour can be of an external and individual nature. External determinants of sustainable behaviour can vary depending on the context and individual factors, but they generally include government regulations and policies that can drive sustainable behaviour through mandates, taxes or financial incentives, such as cost savings or subsidies for sustainable choices. Effective communication and education campaigns may also be positive external motivations to adopt sustainable practices, provided that they are accessible and available (McKenzie, 2008).

The influence of cultural values and country-of-origin factors cannot be underestimated. Combined with the impact of demographic characteristics, they can influence sustainable behaviour. For example, younger generations often prioritise sustainability more than older ones (Wiernik et al., 2013).

With regard to peer and social networks, it should be noted that belonging to communities or social groups (i.e., of friends, family and colleagues) that prioritise sustainability can encourage and reinforce sustainable behaviour. Personal values and attitudes to sustainability and environmental conservation also play a significant role. This is strongly connected with individual motivation, self-efficacy (belief in one's ability to make a difference), personal goals and environmental sensitivity and awareness to understand one's own impact on the environment and society.

On the other hand, some psychological barriers like scepticism, inertia and a perceived lack of impact can hinder sustainable behaviour. Some individuals may perceive sustainability efforts to be too incremental or ineffective in addressing pressing global challenges (Doni et al., 2020). Therefore, providing feedback on personal environmental impacts is crucial and it can encourage behaviour change.

These determinants interact and influence one another, making it essential to consider a holistic approach when encouraging sustainable behaviour. Effective strategies often combine multiple factors, addressing both individual motivations and external influences.

## 3.4 The role of NGOs in a circular economy

NGOs are civic organisations that work on their own initiative to improve and promote the overall well-being of society (Nikkhah & Redzuan, 2010). This philanthropic so-called 'third sector' plays a significant role in promoting sustainability and can advocate sustainable policies at the local, national and international levels (Unerman & O'Dwyer, 2010).

A major challenge for NGOs is environmental education. NGOs raise awareness about sustainability issues with campaigns, workshops and educational programmes. They inform the public about the importance of sustainable practices and their impact on the environment. For example, the U.S.-based *Sierra Club* [https://www.sierraclub.org/explore-issues] advocates environmental conservation. It has been involved in campaigns to promote clean energy, protect public land and raise awareness about climate change, for example, 'Tell Your Senator: It's Time to Act on Wildlife'.

NGOs can engage with governments, businesses and communities to promote environmentally friendly regulations and practices, as well as to leverage resources and expertise for sustainable and conservation initiatives (Liu et al., 2020).

*The Nature Conservancy* [https://www.nature.org/en-us/] is an organisation that works on various conservation projects worldwide. For instance, it has partnered with governments and local communities in Brazil to protect the Amazon Rainforest through sustainable land management and reforestation. In Europe, it helps municipalities utilise existing and new green spaces to manage stormwater, reduce heat island effects and increase biodiversity, to help cities protect their residents from the impacts of a changing climate.

Thanks to their collaborative efforts NGOs can conduct research on environmental issues and collect data to support evidence-based policymaking. Thus, they can provide valuable insights into the state of the environment and the consequences of unsustainable practices.

One such organisation – the *SEI Foundation (Stiftelsen The Stockholm Environment Institute)* [https://www.sei.org/] – is a network of researchers, policymakers and practitioners dedicated to advancing sustainable consumption. Their primary objective is to initiate and conduct studies and other research and disseminate knowledge in the environmental field. Their activities include assessment and development of technologies, policies and related environmental management techniques and strategies for environmentally sustainable social development. They conduct research, organise conferences and collaborate on projects to promote sustainable consumption and production systems. The data they obtain allow them to monitor and report on the progress of sustainability initiatives, thus holding governments and businesses accountable for their commitment to environmental and social responsibility.

For example, international movement *350.org* [https://350.org/about/] organises global climate rallies and campaigns. It plays a pivotal role in the divestment movement, pressuring institutions to withdraw investments from fossil fuel companies.

NGOs can respond to environmental disasters and support communities in building resilience to climate change and other sustainability-related challenges. For example, the global nonprofit organisation *Water.org* [https://water.org/about-us/] addresses the global water crisis by providing access to safe water and sanitation. It partners with local organisations to implement sustainable water and sanitation solutions in communities around the world.

Many NGOs are involved in conservation efforts to protect endangered species, ecosystems and natural resources. One of the best-recognised pro-environmental NGOs is the *World Wide Fund for Nature* [https://www.worldwildlife.org/]. The WWF focuses on conserving wildlife and ecosystems. Together with partners at all levels, it transforms markets and policies towards sustainability, tackles threats driving the climate crisis and protects and restores wildlife and its habitats. It has initiated projects like the 'Living Himalayas Initiative' to promote sustainable development in the Himalayan region, aiming to protect biodiversity while improving livelihoods.

The *Greenpeace Foundation* [https://www.greenpeace.org/poland/] is known for its environmental activism, engaging in direct action to draw attention to environmental issues. It has campaigned against single-use plastic and advocated adopting renewable energy globally. Another such NGO is *Conservation International* [https://www.conservation.org/], which works to protect biodiversity. It has partnered with businesses to promote sustainable supply chains, including efforts to protect coral reefs and support sustainable fisheries. These NGOs are all determined to protect biodiversity and promote sustainable land and resource management.

NGOs empower local communities to adopt sustainable practices, such as organic farming, waste reduction and renewable energy adoption. They often work closely with communities to implement sustainable development projects. For example, the cooperative projects of the international organisation *Prokarde* [https://prokarde.org/] seek to transform realities so that communities and groups of people can improve their situations and expand their future possibilities, thus contributing to their progress and that of the environment, with a particular focus on the education, health, social and promotion of women fields.

An illustration of this is the activities of the *Rainforest Foundation* [https://rainforestfoundation.org/about/mission-history/]. Its branches in the United States, the United Kingdom and Norway work to protect rainforests and the rights of indigenous peoples living in them. They have successfully partnered with indigenous communities in Central and South America to combat deforestation and promote sustainable land use.

Another good example is the *SolarAid* charity [https://solar-aid.org/], the mission of which is to combat poverty and climate change by using solar energy. It provides affordable solar lights in Africa, thus reducing reliance on polluting and unsustainable kerosene lamps.

NGOs as stakeholders in sustainable change often collaborate with businesses to encourage sustainable practices in the private sector. They also provide guidance on environmental and social responsibility and advocate sustainable supply chains. For instance, *Oxfam International* [https://www.oxfam.org/en] addresses social and environmental issues. It works with communities in developing countries to promote sustainable agriculture and provide access to clean water, contributing to both environmental and social sustainability.

Poland also has several organisations dedicated to promoting sustainable consumption and raising awareness about responsible consumer choices. Below are listed a few Polish NGOs that focus on sustainable consumption and introducing circular practices in Poland:

- *Polskie Stowarzyszenie 'Zero Waste'* (The Polish *Zero Waste* Association) [https://zero-waste.pl/o-nas/#nasza-misja] concentrates on reducing waste and promoting responsible consumption. It organises pro-environmental events, provides educational resources and supports individuals, businesses and local communities interested in adopting zero-waste principles.
- Ośrodek Działań Ekologicznych 'sustainable consumption and production patterns.
- ***Polskie Stowarzyszenie Budownictwa Ekologicznego PLGBC* (the Polish Green Building Council)** [https://plgbc.org.pl/] focuses on sustainable building Źródła' (The Centre for Environmental Activities, ŹRÓDŁA) [https://www.zrodla.org/english/] is a nonprofit organisation with a mission to educate students, teachers and the general public about environmental issues and expand their capacity to act for a more sustainable world. It focuses on the intersection between economics and the environment. It conducts research and educational activities to promote construction practices but also emphasises sustainable consumption as part of a broader sustainability agenda in the construction sector. Its mission is to radically transform buildings, cities and their surroundings in such a way that how they are planned, designed, erected, used, retrofitted, demolished and processed is as sustainable as possible.
- *Fundacja 'Ekopotencjał – Przestrzeń Możliwości'* (the Foundation 'Eco-potential – Space of Possibilities') [https://ekopotencjal.pl/] works for widely understood ecological education, environmental protection and sustainable development, and promotes upcycling and circular design practices in Poland. It organises workshops and events and collaborates with designers and artists to raise awareness about creative ways to repurpose materials.
- *Stowarzyszenie Ekologiczne EKO-UNIA* (the EKO-UNIA Ecological Association) [https://eko-unia.org.pl/en/] works on various environmental issues, including sustainable consumption and waste reduction. It organises education programmes, campaigns and initiatives to encourage eco-conscious choices. It provides local communities with access to information and gives competent legal advice concerning various investments that threaten the natural environment. In this way, it supports

citizens' right to co-decide on local issues such as opencast mining, wind farms, atomic power stations and coal-fired stations.

- The *Fundacja Nasza Ziemia (Our Earth Foundation)* [https://www.naszaziemia.pl/english/] aims to raise the level of public environmental awareness, strengthen the sense of responsibility for the environment and encourage actions to protect it. It realises projects in four areas: waste management; saving and protecting natural resources; protecting and preserving biodiversity; and environmental education.
- The *Fundacja Kupuj Odpowiedzialnie* **(Buy Responsibly Foundation)** [https://ekonsument.pl/s56_what_we_do.html] promotes responsible and ethical consumption choices, including fair trade products and sustainable consumer behaviour. It is a Polish organisation focusing on sustainable development and environmental protection, responsible consumption and production, and respect for human rights and environmental principles in business.
- The *Fundacja Zielony Ład (*Green Deal Foundation) [https://www.fundacjazielonylad.pl/] focuses on environmental education and promotes sustainable living practices in Poland. The foundation promotes knowledge and actions for environmental protection, and the idea of sustainable development (e.g., a sustainable economy, agriculture, mobility, transport, food chain and production cycles). It organises competitions and artistic, cultural and sports events that promote environmentally friendly attitudes and organises festivals and art events related to environmental protection.
- The *Koalicja Klimatyczna* (Climate Coalition) [https://koalicjaklimatyczna.org/o-nas]. While not exclusively dedicated to sustainable consumption, this coalition of 26 NGOs in Poland works on climate change-related issues, including the promotion of sustainable and low-carbon lifestyles. The coalition carries out a variety of activities, from monitoring legislative work at the national and European levels to organising conferences and workshops for various audiences – business representatives, politicians and journalists – to educational activities aimed at children and young people.
- The *Polish Circular Hotspot* [http://circularhotspot.pl/en/hotspot] is a platform that brings together various stakeholders, including businesses, NGOs and government agencies, to promote a circular economy in Poland. Thanks to cooperation and access to shared resources, they can achieve more both for the introduction of a circular economy and for their own interests. They organise events and workshops and provide resources to support the transition to circular practices.
- The *Fundacja Instytut na Rzecz Ekorozwoju* (Institute for Sustainable Development) [https://www.pine.org.pl/english/] is a non-governmental think-tank-type organisation that acts for various sustainability issues, including circularity. It conducts research and projects to promote eco-friendly and circular practices in Poland. The Institute for Sustainable

> Development works to promote and implement principles and solutions which contribute to sustainable development in Poland. In its activities, the Institute is guided by its mission to build positive relations between socio-economic development and environmental protection and to act in the interests of present and future generations.

These are just a few examples of the diverse ways in which NGOs are actively engaged in promoting sustainability in Poland. NGOs in Poland contribute to ongoing efforts to raise awareness about sustainable consumption, reduce environmental impacts and promote responsible choices among consumers and businesses in the country.

While NGOs often act with noble aims, it is important to acknowledge that not all activities conducted by NGOs are universally beneficial, and there can be instances in which their actions might be counterproductive or controversial. Advocacy efforts by these organisations may not always lead to the desired policy changes or outcomes due to complex political and economic factors. In some cases, NGOs may even be accused of meddling in the political affairs of a country, which can lead to tensions with governments and hinder their ability to achieve their aims (Epperly & Lee, 2015).

NGOs operating in different regions or countries may inadvertently impose Western-centric solutions or fail to consider local customs and traditions, leading to cultural insensitivity and backlashes from local communities. It can happen that well-intentioned projects conducted by NGOs may have unintended negative consequences. For example, introducing a new agricultural technique may inadvertently harm local ecosystems or disrupt traditional livelihoods.

Controversies surrounding the activities of the philanthropic sector tend to be linked to overemphasis on fundraising. Some NGOs may prioritise fundraising over their mission, leading to an over-reliance on emotional appeals or sensationalism in their communications to attract donors. In cases in which multiple NGOs are involved in a particular issue, there can be competition for resources and attention, potentially leading to fragmentation and inefficiency in addressing problems.

In addition, certain NGOs may spend a significant proportion of their funds on administration or overheads, which can limit the impact of their projects.

Furthermore, some NGOs may have financial or political motivations that conflict with their stated aims. For instance, an environmental NGO receiving substantial funding from a particular industry might be less inclined to challenge practices in that industry (Poret, 2019).

Obviously, these allegations are not specific to environmental organisations, but they are worth mentioning here because they provide a broader perspective on sustainable advocacy.

It is essential to recognise that the 'third sector' is diverse, and the impact of any organisation can vary widely. NGOs should continually evaluate their methods, collaborate with local stakeholders and maintain transparency and accountability to minimise counterproductive activities and maximise their positive contributions to sustainability. Therefore donors, media and the public should critically assess the effectiveness and ethics of NGOs in their pursuit of sustainability goals.

Overall, NGOs have a multifaceted role in promoting sustainability, encompassing advocacy, education, research and direct action to address environmental and social issues.

## 3.5 The corporate sector and its involvement in sustainable change

While the pursuit of profit by the corporate sector can sometimes conflict with sustainability goals, there is growing recognition that long-term profitability is intertwined with environmental and social responsibility. Many companies are embracing sustainability as a core part of their business strategy, recognising that it benefits both their bottom line and the planet. Thus, the corporate sector plays a pivotal role in driving sustainability and addressing global challenges.

Business organisations are important stakeholders in sustainable change for several reasons.

*Economic impact*: corporations are major contributors to a country's economy. Their practices, whether sustainable or not, can have a significant impact on employment, gross domestic product (GDP) and overall economic well-being. Sustainable corporate practices can lead to economic growth, which benefits society. Since businesses lead in innovation and technological development, they can create and adopt sustainable technologies, products and processes which can drive positive change across industries (Green Production Guide, 2016). Furthermore, sustainable practices in the corporate sector can lead to job creation in sectors like renewable energy, sustainable agriculture and green technologies, contributing to employment opportunities.

*Global reach*: multinational corporations have a global presence and can influence sustainability practices in multiple countries. They can set sustainability standards that extend beyond national boundaries. This is also related to the global supply chains that many corporations use. By implementing sustainability standards and practices throughout these supply chains, they can influence the environmental and social impact of their products.

*Consumer influence*: businesses have a direct influence on consumer choices. When they offer sustainable products and educate consumers about their benefits, they can steer consumer behaviour towards more environmentally friendly options. It is obvious that businesses are significant consumers of natural resources, energy and water. Responsible use of these resources, introducing environmentally friendly manufacturing techniques and eco-friendly packaging, promoting recycling and up-cycling and adopting these solutions in business practices increase customer confidence and contribute to consumer acceptance of the sustainable solutions being disseminated (Hollo, 2014). An organisation worth mentioning is The Consumer Goods Forum (CGF) [https://www.theconsumergoodsforum.com/]. This organisation is a global platform that brings together consumer goods companies and retailers to work on sustainability issues, including sustainable consumption. They focus on topics such as reducing food waste and promoting responsible sourcing and product design.

Many corporations recognise their social and environmental responsibilities. While governments frequently impose regulations and standards, corporations might help ensure environmental preservation and social well-being by complying with these regulations and even exceeding them through sustainable practices.

Businesses engage in philanthropy, support community initiatives and participate in partnerships to address sustainability challenges. One manifestation of such positive attitudes is 'Extended Producer Responsibility' (EPR). This is a policy approach used in waste management and environmental protection which shifts responsibility for managing the lifecycle of products and packaging from consumers and local governments to the manufacturers and producers of these products (Cai & Choi, 2019).

Under EPR, manufacturers are legally responsible for the collection and safe disposal of their products and packaging after use by consumers, taking responsibility for their products from product design to waste collection and recycling programmes. This can involve setting up collection points or partnering with existing recycling facilities. EPR encourages producers to design cleaner more durable products that are easier to recycle or dispose of safely and to minimise the environmental impact of products throughout their lifecycle.

EPR policies vary by region and product type, so the specifics can differ from place to place. Some countries have comprehensive EPR laws covering a wide range of products, while others focus on specific categories like electronics or packaging materials (Pouikli, 2020). In some cases, the financial responsibility of manufacturers results in paying fees or taxes to support recycling and waste management programmes. These funds are then used to cover the cost of collecting and recycling their products.

EPR is seen as an effective way to incentivise producers to make products that are easier to recycle and to reduce the environmental impact of products and packaging. It also helps shift the financial burden of waste management away from taxpayers and local governments and puts it on the businesses that create the products in the first place.

Unfortunately, the impact of the corporate sector, and manufacturing companies in particular, in terms of sustainability is not exclusively positive. The biggest threat to the environment and sustainable consumption is planned product obsolescence (Ryś & Prymon-Ryś, 2017). This is manufacturers reducing the lifespan of products in order to induce consumers to replace goods more often. Instead of improving the technical quality of the product and introducing an upcycling approach, customers are offered an improved quality of service and an expanded sphere of consumer experiences and emotions. Planned product obsolescence is a manufacturing strategy to design goods in such a way that they have a limited useful life, and when this period expires they become inoperable and often uneconomical to repair (Ryś, 2015).

Observing manufacturing enterprise practices makes it possible to identify several forms of planned ageing of products (Ryś, 2015; Ryś & Prymon-Ryś, 2017), which are as follows:

- using components with less durability, resulting in a shorter product lifetime;
- intentionally building in mechanisms to limit the lifespan of the product;
- failing to manufacture replacement parts, discontinuing technical support and not offering software updates for older versions of computer programs or operating systems;
- making repairs more difficult through the use of designs or assembly components that prevent the customer from repairing the equipment himself. This includes failing to make technical specifications (such as manuals and electronic layouts) public;
- planned restriction of the usefulness of cheaper versions of a product by, for example, using a simplified version of the software or blocking selected features that will be activated when buying up-scale equipment (in the automotive industry);
- planned obsolescence involving the creation of non-reusable products. The positive aspect of this approach is that materials have been improved and the cost of manufacturing products has been reduced, which has allowed their prices to fall to such a level that their one-time use is cost-effective (e.g., for medical applications). However, this category also includes examples of products the single use of which is no longer so obvious and necessary, which contributes to increasing the amount of electronic waste, which is difficult to recycle);
- planned product obsolescence involving the creation of consumer wants to be associated with the launch of new product versions with new functional and aesthetic solutions. Customers are encouraged to get rid of older products, the physical exhaustion of which has not yet occurred and which could still be successfully used, to replace them with new fashionable models.

The mentioned above that planned product obsolescence is not an unambiguous phenomenon, and that the motives for this type of practice vary. Many cases of planned obsolescence were and are driven by EU legislation, such as the order to withdraw traditional incandescent light bulbs from sale (Ryś, 2015). Increasingly, one can observe the practice of shortening the life cycle of a product to ensure that a company increases its sales volume in a saturated market.

In the context of the pursuit of a circular economy, entrepreneurs who undertake such practices are counterproductive stakeholders in sustainable change.

Both NGOs and enterprises (businesses) play vital roles in advancing the concept and implementation of a circular economy, and it is challenging to categorically say one is more important than the other. Their roles are complementary (see Table 3.1).

*Table 3.1* The roles of businesses and NGOs in implementing sustainable change

| *Corporate sector (businesses)* | | *Philanthropic sector (NGOs)* | |
|---|---|---|---|
| *Impact* | *Explanation* | *Impact* | *Explanation* |
| Innovation and implementation | Businesses are at the forefront of developing and implementing circular economy practices. They drive innovation in product design, manufacturing processes and supply chains to reduce waste and resource consumption. | Advocacy and awareness | NGOs often advocate policy changes and promote awareness of the importance of circular economy principles among governments, businesses and the public. |
| Market transformation | Enterprises can bring circular products and services to the mass market, thereby accelerating the adoption of circular practices. | Research and education | NGOs conduct research on circular economy practices, sharing knowledge and best practices with businesses and policymakers. |
| Economic impact | Circular economy initiatives can lead to cost savings, increased competitiveness and new revenue streams for businesses. | Monitoring and accountability | NGOs can hold businesses and governments accountable for their circular economy commitments, ensuring they follow through on sustainability goals. |
| Job creation | Transitioning to a circular economy can generate jobs in sectors like recycling, repairing and remanufacturing. | Community engagement | NGOs work with local communities to promote circular practices at the grassroots level, encouraging sustainable consumer behaviour. |

*Source*: Authors.

In summary, enterprises are essential to drive the practical implementation of circular economy principles, while NGOs play a crucial role in advocacy, education, research and monitoring to create an enabling environment for a circular economy to thrive. A successful transition to a circular economy often involves collaboration between these two sectors, along with government involvement, to create a more sustainable and resource-efficient future.

## 3.6 Educators, academics and researchers promoting a circular economy

Solving sustainability challenges requires a collective effort involving various academic and educational organisations. Universities and other research institutions contribute through research, innovation and education. They develop sustainable technologies, conduct environmental studies and train the next generation of sustainability leaders. Organisations focused on technological advancement, like Wärtsilä's Sustainable Technology Hub (STH) [https://www.sustainabletechnologyhub.com/] and the Sustainability & Innovation Hub Evoqua [https://www.evoqua.com/en-150/], can develop and promote sustainable solutions, such as renewable energy technologies, water purification methods and sustainable agriculture practices.

In the context of the circular economy, which is seen as a crucial framework for addressing environmental, economic and social issues, several main research trends and areas of focus may be distinguished (Camacho-Otero et al., 2018; Ferasso et al., 2020; Goyal et al., 2021).

*Circular business models*: there is growing interest in circular business models, such as product-as-a-service, sharing platforms and take-back systems. Researchers are investigating the feasibility and scalability of these models.

*Sustainable supply chains*: research is exploring ways to create more sustainable and circular supply chains. This involves studying procurement practices, sustainable sourcing and supply chain transparency.

*Circular design and innovation*: research is focusing on developing new product design strategies that prioritise reuse, repairing and recycling. This includes exploring materials, technologies and business models that enable circular product lifecycles.

*The circular economy and digital technologies*: integration of digital technologies like blockchain, the Internet of Things (IoT) and artificial intelligence (AI) in circular economy practices is a research area.

*Consumer behaviour and circular consumption*: understanding consumer behaviour and motivations for adopting circular practices, such as product repair and reuse, is a topic of interest. Researchers are studying consumer perceptions and barriers to circular consumption.

*Waste reduction and recycling technologies*: investigating advanced recycling technologies, such as chemical recycling and upcycling, to reduce waste and enhance resource recovery is a research focus.

*Policy and regulation*: research is examining the role of government policies and regulations in promoting circular economy practices. This includes studying EPR schemes and circular economy legislation.

*Circular cities*: there is a trend towards researching circular economy strategies at the urban level. This involves exploring circular urban planning, waste management and sustainable infrastructure.

*The circular economy in industry sectors*: researchers are examining how circular economy principles can be applied to specific industries, such as fashion, electronics and automotives, to reduce environmental impacts and enhance sustainability.

*The circular economy in developing countries*: research is looking into how circular economy concepts can be adapted to the specific challenges and opportunities in developing countries.

*Circular economy education and awareness*: there is growing emphasis on educating future professionals and the public about circular economy principles, including circular design thinking and sustainable consumption.

*Circular economy metrics*: there is a research trend in developing metrics and frameworks to measure and assess the circularity of products and processes. Researchers aim to create standardised indicators for circularity assessments.

It is important to note that research trends can evolve, as the field of circular economy is dynamic and continually changing. Researchers and practitioners in this field continue to explore innovative solutions to address sustainability challenges.

Above all, the key impact of academic institutions as sustainable stakeholders is in education. They help individuals understand the environmental, social and economic consequences of their consumption choices. People become more mindful consumers as a result of being educated about concerns such as resource depletion, climate change and social equity. Educated individuals are more likely to engage in sustainable innovation, whether in business, technology or policymaking. They can contribute to the development of eco-friendly products and services.

Educational institutions create future leaders who can shape industries, organisations and governments with a strong commitment to sustainability at the local, national and global levels. With their long-term perspective on sustainability, education encourages people to consider the impact of their actions on future generations and the planet, leading to more responsible consumption patterns. At the micro level, education campaigns can inspire individuals to change their consumption behaviour. When people are informed about sustainable alternatives and the benefits they bring, they are more likely to make environmentally friendly choices.

While education alone may not solve all sustainability challenges, it is a foundational component. It equips individuals with the knowledge, skills and mindset needed to make informed choices and drive meaningful change towards a more sustainable future.

Educational institutions can play a significant role in promoting sustainable consumption in various ways, which are as follows:

- including sustainability and environmental topics in the curriculum across disciplines;
- fostering innovation for more eco-friendly products and services;
- organising awareness events, workshops and seminars;
- implementing sustainable practices in universities and campuses (e.g., energy-efficient buildings, waste reduction, food sharing and eco-friendly transport options);
- engaging students in sustainability initiatives and projects;
- creating real-world learning opportunities and internships for students, thanks to collaboration with businesses and organisations committed to sustainability;
- procuring sustainably: making responsible purchasing decisions, opting for eco-friendly products and services when possible;
- sharing knowledge and encouraging sustainable behaviour by extending green initiatives to the local community;
- monitoring and reporting the progress of institutions towards sustainability goals, promoting transparency and accountability.

By actively engaging in these activities, educational institutions can not only educate the next generation but also contribute to a more sustainable and environmentally responsible society.

## 3.7 The importance of influencers and celebrity endorsement

The characteristics of modern consumers result in a greater importance of influencers and celebrities in introducing sustainable consumption. In the last few years, there has been a growing trend of involvement of all types of prominent figures: politicians, journalists, artists and athletes, many of whom have become influencers on widely known social media platforms. These people are celebrities, which is defined as 'the state of being famous, especially in the entertainment business' (Goodman et al., 2017). Influencers and celebrities often have large followings on social media, allowing them to reach millions of people quickly. When they promote sustainable products or practices, it can lead to widespread awareness. Thanks to their informative and creative content, they influence consumer choices, explaining why sustainable practices are important and how they can be incorporated in everyday life.

Many people trust the recommendations of their favourite influencers or pop idols. Therefore, when these individuals endorse sustainable brands or lifestyles, it lends credibility to the cause. Celebrities, in particular, are trendsetters.

Their fans tend to replicate their actions when they embrace sustainable practices or advocate eco-friendly businesses. Therefore, many brands collaborate with influencers and celebrities in marketing campaigns to drive consumer interest and adoption. Apart from marketing activities, some influencers and celebrities actively engage in pro-environmental advocacy and activism. They use their platforms to raise awareness about green issues, which can lead to sustainable change. However, it is essential to ensure that these influencers and celebrities genuinely align with sustainability values and practices rather than just engaging in 'greenwashing' for publicity. Authenticity and a genuine commitment to sustainability are crucial for the success of their efforts.

In the realm of sustainability and eco-conscious content, influencers can be categorised into two groups based on their focus and content: *environmental activists* and *lifestyle influencers*. Some influencers who are actively involved in environmental advocacy and campaigns use their platforms to raise awareness about pressing environmental issues. Among them one can distinguish the following:

- *Zero-Waste Influencers*, who advocate minimising waste generation through practices like bulk shopping, composting and reducing single-use plastic. Bea Johnson (@zerowastehome) is a leading voice in the zero-waste movement. She has popularised the concept of a zero-waste lifestyle through her blog and books, inspiring people to reduce waste and consume more consciously. Lauren Singer (@trashusfortossers) is another influential figure in the zero-waste community. She founded the blog 'Trash is for Tossers' and a sustainable product line called 'Package Free'. Her efforts encourage sustainable consumption and waste reduction. In Poland, Joanna Kądziołka (Polish Association Zero Waste) is a prominent figure in the zero-waste and sustainable living community. She shares practical tips and advice on reducing waste and living an eco-friendlier lifestyle through her blog and social media.
- *Wildlife and nature conservationists* advocate for all species. They create and share content about protecting the environment on social media or have actively taken on a conservation role. One of the first and most recognised advocates of wildlife conservancy was Dr. Jane Goodall. She spent decades protecting chimpanzees and inspiring people to conserve nature. Currently, her work is being continued by The Jane Goodall Institute (https://janegoodall.org/), a global non-profit wildlife and environment conservation organisation. The institute's missions are to improve the treatment and understanding of primates through public education and legal representation, to protect their habitats in partnership with local communities and to recruit and train young people for these missions. The supermodel Gisele Bündchen (@gisele) has used her platform to raise awareness about the role of the circular economy in protecting rainforests. She has advocated sustainable agriculture and responsible sourcing of forest products

to reduce deforestation. In addition to using her social networks to share information about different subjects related to the importance of preserving all forms of life, Bündchen also attended a meeting to discuss the matter at the United Nations. Another celebrity, Leonardo DiCaprio, is well-known for his commitment to environmental causes, including circular economy principles. He founded the 'Leonardo DiCaprio Foundation' (https://foundationguide.org/foundations/leonardo-dicaprio-foundation/), which supports projects focused on wildlife conservation, renewable energy and responsible consumption. Adrian Grenier (@adriangrenier), an actor known for his role in 'Entourage', founded the 'Lonely Whale' foundation, which focuses on ocean conservation. He promotes a circular economy by advocating reducing single-use plastics and recycling ocean plastics.

- *Climate Change Activists.* Some influencers specifically address climate change issues, providing information on climate science, policy and advocacy efforts. Among the most recognised is Greta Thunberg (@gretathunberg), a young climate activist known for her powerful speeches and advocacy for urgent climate action. She has inspired millions of people worldwide to adopt more sustainable lifestyles and reduce their carbon footprint.
- *Environmental Educators.* These influencers aim to educate their audience about various environmental topics, from responsible consumer choices to renewable energy, for example, Kasia Worek (@kateebag), a sustainability educator who shares insights into ecological awareness and helps environmental education. Marcin Popkiewicz (https://instytutsprawobywatelskich.pl/) is a megatrends analyst, expert and journalist covering links in the areas of economy, energy, resources and the environment.
- *Ethical Business and Entrepreneurship Influencers.* These highlight businesses and entrepreneurs who prioritise sustainability and social responsibility. These influencers and platforms often share insights, stories and resources related to sustainable entrepreneurship. Ethical Influencers (@ethicalinfluencers) is a collective of influencers committed to promoting ethical and sustainable living, including businesses with ethical practices. There are also individual influencers like Francesca Willow (@ethicalunicorn), who shares content related to ethical living, sustainable fashion and responsible business practices, and Jayn Sterland (@jaynsterland), the Managing Director of Weleda UK, who advocates sustainable business practices, particularly in the beauty and wellness industry. In Poland, Natalia Hatalska (https://infuture.institute/natalia-hatalska/) is a renowned expert on CSR and sustainable business practices. She educates businesses and individuals on sustainable consumption and ethical business behaviour. She has been recognised as one of the 50 most influential women in Poland and twice recognised in the 'Who does Polish business listen to?' poll as one of the 10 most important authorities in Polish business.
- *Community and NGO Collaborators* are influencers who partner with environmental organisations and NGOs or local authorities to promote their

causes and initiatives. Oleśnica: Miasto Zero Waste (Oleśnica: Zero Waste City) [https://olesnica.naszemiasto.pl/tag/zero-waste] is a good example of such collaboration. It is a city in Poland that has gained recognition for its commitment to becoming a low-impact community. Local influencers, activists and government officials have been actively involved in promoting sustainable consumption practices in the region.

*Eco-lifestyle influencers* promote sustainable living practices in daily life, such as reducing waste, using eco-friendly products and adopting green home practices. They often advocate sustainable consumption and responsible consumer behaviour. For example, Paul Hawken (https://paulhawken.com/) is an environmentalist and author of the book 'Drawdown', which outlines practical solutions for reducing carbon emissions. He promotes sustainable consumption as a key element in addressing climate change.

More specific forms of sustainable advocacy include the following:

- *Eco-Fashion Influencers* promote sustainable and ethical fashion choices, emphasising clothing made from eco-friendly materials and ethical manufacturing practices. Emma Watson (@emmawatson), known for her role as Hermione in the Harry Potter series, has been an advocate for sustainable fashion. She has been a supporter of 'Good On You' (https://goodonyou.eco/emma-watson-good-on-you-supporter/) a popular resource that rates fashion brands based on their commitment to sustainability and transparency. This partnership showcases how celebrities can actively engage in circular fashion initiatives. Her approach emphasises the importance of extending the lifespan of clothing. Livia Firth is a co-founder of Eco-Age (https://eco-age.com/resources/author/livia-firth/), a sustainability consultancy, and an advocate for sustainable fashion. She promotes ethical and sustainable practices in the fashion industry and encourages consumers to make mindful clothing choices.
- *Outdoor and Adventure Influencers* and *Sustainable Travel Influencers* are people who love the outdoors and promote environmental conservation and responsible outdoor activities like hiking, camping and wildlife conservation. These influencers focus on eco-friendly travel practices, including sustainable tourism, responsible wildlife encounters and reducing the carbon footprint of travel. Several influencers and celebrities may be mentioned here: Kiersten Rich (@theblondeabroad), who shares her travel experiences and promotes sustainable travel practices, eco-friendly accommodation and responsible tourism; Evelina Eco warrior (@0earthwanderess), who is a sustainable travel blogger who focuses on eco-friendly travel tips, responsible tourism and adventure; and Jonathan Irish (@jonathan_irish), who is a conservation photographer and who shares his outdoor adventures promoting responsible travel and environmental stewardship.

- *Green Beauty and Skincare Influencers*. Advocating clean and eco-friendly beauty products, these influencers emphasise natural and sustainable skincare and makeup choices. There are many examples: Organic Beauty Blogger (@organicbunny) shares her journey in green beauty and promotes organic and non-toxic skincare and beauty products; Amber George (@ambertheevegan) shares her expertise in green beauty, skincare routines and natural product recommendations; Brandie Gilliam (@thoughtfullymagazine) is founder of 'Thoughtfully Magazine', a women's lifestyle publication which focuses on conscious clean living, including green beauty and skincare; and Suzi Swope (@gurlgonegreen) is a green beauty blogger and advocate who shares her experiences with clean beauty products and skincare routines.
- *DIY and Upcycling Influencers* and *Minimalist Lifestyle Influencers*. These influencers showcase DIY projects and upcycling ideas to encourage recycling and repurposing materials. They promote simplicity and minimal consumption, which often aligns with sustainable living principles. Rob Greenfield (@robjgreenfield) is an environmental activist known for his extreme sustainability challenges, like living a year without producing any rubbish. His campaigns raise awareness of the environmental impact of our consumption habits.
- *Vegan and Plant-Based Influencers* focus on promoting a vegan or plant-based lifestyle, highlighting the environmental benefits of plant-based diets and sustainable food choices. Immy Lucas (@sustainably_vegan) promotes sustainable and vegan lifestyle practices, encourages reducing waste and aims to raise awareness about environmental issues. This aligns with circular economy principles by promoting a diet that reduces waste and resource consumption.
- *Sustainable Parenting Influencers* focus on eco-conscious parenting practices and share tips on raising children with sustainability in mind. For example, Lauren and Daniel Singer, known as the Sustainable Duo (@sustainable_duo), share their journey towards a sustainable lifestyle, including sustainable parenting. They provide tips on eco-friendly practices for families. Another illustration is Catrina (@plantedfamilies), who promotes plant-based eco-friendly living for families. She shares insights into sustainable parenting, plant-based recipes and eco-conscious choices.

It is important to note that many influencers may fit in more than one of these categories, and some may have a broader focus on sustainability in general. The diversity of influencers reflects the multifaceted nature of sustainability and the different aspects of it that individuals can contribute to.

Good circular economy influencers possess several key qualities and practices that are essential to effectively promote sustainable circular practices. First, they have a thorough understanding of the circular economy concept, its principles and its benefits. This knowledge allows them to create informative and engaging content that explains the circular economy concept, showcases real-world examples and provides actionable tips for adopting circular practices. To make the circular economy relatable and emotionally engaging they share personal experiences and success stories and thus are particularly effective (Anderson, 2011).

Successful sustainable influencers maintain a positive and hopeful outlook, emphasising the opportunities and benefits of the circular economy rather than focusing solely on the challenges. They make circular economy practices accessible to a broad audience by breaking down complex concepts into actionable steps that anyone can take. To achieve sustainable goals, they constantly stay in touch with their audience, answering questions, fostering discussion and creating a sense of community around circular economy topics (Moser, 2016).

In order to create compelling and engaging content, these influencers stay informed about the latest developments and trends in the circular economy, adapt their content and strategies as necessary and encourage innovation in circular solutions, whether it is in product design, recycling methods or business models, and share these innovations with their followers (Hollo, 2014).

Not only innovative solutions but also traditional and genuine products are among their interests. They highlight and support businesses and brands that prioritise circular economy principles, helping their audience discover sustainable options.

The main features of sustainable influencers include the following:

- authenticity (to genuinely believe in and practice circular economy principles in their own lives or businesses);
- transparency (about their own efforts and challenges in adopting circular practices, making them more relatable to the audience);
- advocacy for policy changes (and industry regulations that promote circular practices on a broader scale);
- a long-term commitment (understanding that transitioning to a circular economy is a gradual process and remaining committed to the cause);
- a measurable impact (tracking and sharing the measurable impact of their circular practices and campaigns, demonstrating positive environmental and economic outcomes);
- collaboration (with other influencers, experts and organisations in the sustainability and circular economy space to amplify their impact and bring diverse perspectives).

A good circular economy influencer should inspire and empower their audience to embrace circular practices in their personal lives, businesses and communities. Their influence should contribute to the transition to a more sustainable and circular future.

However, involving celebrities in promoting sustainability can have both positive and negative results. One potential threat is greenwashing: celebrities might endorse products or initiatives that appear sustainable but are not genuinely environmentally friendly (Rimmer, 2012). Superficial or short-term engagement can mislead the public and undermine real sustainability efforts. Celebrities may lack expertise in sustainability or oversimplify complex issues, leading to inaccurate information and potentially harmful recommendations. Relying heavily on celebrities for environmental promotion can be risky, as their involvement may not be sustained or reliable. Sometimes, the focus can shift from the cause itself to the celebrity's personal brand, detracting attention from the sustainability message. Celebrities may be unreliable, constantly switching causes or endorsements, making long-term involvement in sustainability efforts difficult. To mitigate these dangers, it is essential for sustainability campaigns to involve credible experts, use evidence-based messaging and focus on substantive actions rather than just celebrity endorsements.

Nevertheless, some potential risks are inevitable in any marketing activities. Influencers and celebrities effectively use their influence to promote circular economy principles by raising awareness, supporting sustainable practices and collaborating with brands that prioritise circularity and responsible consumption (Moser, 2016). These stakeholders are positive forces in society. They encourage individuals and businesses to make more environmentally responsible choices. Their actions go beyond mere endorsement, often involving personal commitment, expertise and passion for a more sustainable future.

## 3.8 Other sustainable stakeholders

There are other stakeholders in sustainable change that significantly contribute to dissemination and acceptance of the idea of sustainable consumption.

*Governments at the local, national and global levels* play a crucial role in creating and enforcing regulations and policies that promote sustainability. They set emission reduction targets, implement environmental protection and support renewable energy initiatives (Jager & O'Riordan, 2019).

Poland can access funding through various *European Union programmes* and initiatives, such as Horizon Europe, the LIFE Programme and the European Regional Development Fund (ERDF), which support circular economy projects and innovations (Delbeke & Vis, 2015).

In addition, government agencies and international organisations may offer financial rewards or grants to support circular economy initiatives and research.

In today's dynamic world, developing pro-ecological initiatives and projects is becoming a priority for both governments and society. Poland, an integral part of the EU, participates in global efforts to protect the environment and achieve sustainable development. There are many government and social programmes, both national and EU and European, that support pro-ecological market development and can support the implementation of sustainable marketing practices and a circular economy (see Table 3.2).

*Table 3.2* Overview of Polish, EU and European government and social programmes supporting pro-ecological market development.

| *Programme name* | *Programme scope* |
|---|---|
| **Poland** | |
| GreenEvo – Ecological Technology Accelerator | An initiative promoting pro-ecological innovations and supporting developing companies in the ecological sector. |
| 'Ecoinnovacje' programme | A Ministry of Development, Labour and Technology initiative that supports pro-ecological innovations in the industrial and service sectors. |
| 'Mój Prąd' programme | Supports the installation of low-emission energy sources, such as photovoltaic panels, by reducing the cost associated with these investments. |
| 'Prosument' programme | A programme supporting producers of energy from renewable sources, such as photovoltaic installations, with various types of subsidies and preferential loans. |
| Operational Infrastructure and Environment programme | The aim is to support pro-ecological investment in areas such as environmental protection, renewable energy, public transport, water management and so on. |
| Priority 'Czyste Powietrze' programme | Dedicated to improving the energy efficiency of residential buildings by replacing heat sources and thermal modernisation. |
| National Fund for Environmental Protection and Water Management programmes | Various grant and loan programmes supporting pro-ecological projects, including subsidies for photovoltaics, thermal modernisation of buildings and nature protection. |
| **European Union and Europe** | |
| European Green Deal | This is a strategic European Union initiative that aims to achieve climate neutrality by 2050 and promote sustainable development. |
| European Investment Bank | The EIB provides financial support for pro-ecological projects, including investment in renewable energy sources, energy efficiency and environmental protection. |
| European Fund for Regional Development | This fund provides financial support for projects related to improving energy efficiency, sustainable transport and other pro-ecological areas. |
| Just Transition Fund | This initiative aims to support regions that require transformation due to phasing out of coal and other pro-environmental projects. |
| Reconstruction Plan for Europe | In response to the impact of the COVID-19 pandemic, the EU launched this plan to invest in sustainable development, including renewable energy sources, digital transformation and environmental protection. |
| Connecting Europe Facility | A programme financing infrastructure projects in the areas of transport, energy and telecommunications, with an emphasis on sustainable development and integration of energy markets. |

(*Continued*)

*Table 3.2* (Continued)

| *Programme name* | *Programme scope* |
|---|---|
| LIFE programme | An EU programme supporting pro-ecological projects in the areas of nature conservation, resource management, energy efficiency and innovation. |
| Sustainable Development Programme | This focuses on promoting sustainable development in areas such as energy, transport and the economy. |
| NER 300 programme | An EU programme supporting investment in demonstration projects in the area of low-carbon technologies, such as renewable energy and carbon capture and storage (CCS) technologies. |
| EFTA and Norwegian Financial Mechanism programmes | Norway, Iceland and Liechtenstein make funds available to EU countries through these mechanisms that support pro-ecological projects, including environmental protection and energy efficiency. |
| European Environment Agency programmes | These support research, monitoring and environmental protection activities in Europe. |
| Horizon 2020 and Horizon Europe programmes | Programmes financing research and innovation in pro-ecological areas, including low-emission technologies and renewable energy sources. |
| UN and other international organisation programmes | International initiatives such as the United Nations Development Programme and the UN Environment Programme provide support for pro-ecological projects, especially in developing countries. |

*Source*: Authors.

Bodies like the *United Nations* in collaboration with national governments coordinate global efforts to address sustainability challenges. They set global goals (e.g., the Sustainable Development Goals) and provide funding and support for sustainable development projects. Banks, investment firms and venture capitalists can direct funding and investment to sustainable projects and technologies. They can encourage businesses to adopt sustainable practices by providing incentives and financing.

While governments and the other previously mentioned stakeholders influence sustainability at the global or regional level, *grassroots organisations* **and** *community groups* often play a vital role in driving sustainability initiatives at the local level. They engage with communities to promote sustainable practices and environmental conservation.

Collaboration for long-term change is essential for success. Building partnerships with like-minded organisations and stakeholders can lead to mutually beneficial rewards in the circular economy arena. A good illustration of this is ICLEI (Local Governments for Sustainability) [https://iclei.org/], a global network of local governments and cities committed to sustainability. They work on various environmental issues, including sustainable consumption at the local level, through initiatives like the One Planet City Challenge.

The Catholic Church and other religious organizations play a significant role in shaping environmental attitudes among their faithful followers. Pope Francis, in his encyclical, *Laudato Si* (Francis, 2015) emphasizes the importance of caring for our common home, highlighting the interconnectedness of environmental, social and economic issues. The collective influence of religious entities fosters a broader awareness of environmental issues and inspires individuals to integrate ecological considerations into their lifestyles, reflecting a harmonious relationship between faith and environmental responsibility.

Ultimately, the *media* (traditional and digital) can raise awareness about sustainability issues and educate the public about how they can contribute to solving these challenges. For instance, the newsletter *Heated* about the climate crisis [https://heated.world/about] shares insights into sustainable business practices and environmental activism. *Heated* seeks to help readers understand that the climate crisis is not solely a problem of emissions but a problem of culture, economics, media and democracy.

Companies often use media platforms and broadcast channels to create and conduct advertising campaigns that highlight their environmentally friendly products or practices. For example, a car manufacturer might promote its electric vehicle (EV) line to emphasise sustainability. In addition, brands use social media platforms to engage with environmentally conscious consumers. They share sustainability initiatives, provide eco-friendly tips and encourage discussion about environmental issues. They also use blogs, videos and other educational content to inform consumers about sustainability. This content can range from recycling guides to tips for reducing carbon footprints. For example, TriplePundit [https://www.triplepundit.com/] is a media platform that covers sustainable business news and trends, making it a valuable resource for sustainable entrepreneurs. It focuses 'on hard-hitting, evidence-based solutions and journalism for environmental sustainability'.

Some brands create platforms or apps that allow customers to track their own sustainability efforts and compete with others. These platforms can serve as marketing tools while encouraging sustainable actions.

In Poland there are various bodies and organisations that provide rewards and recognition for circular economy efforts. For example, the Ministry of Climate and Environment (Ministerstwo Klimatu i Środowiska) is involved in environmental policies and sustainability initiatives. It offers awards and funding for projects that align with circular economy goals. In addition, municipalities and regional authorities in Poland provide rewards and incentives for circular economy projects and initiatives at the local level.

Apart from regulations and funding programmes, governments also provide marketing incentives as mechanisms to encourage businesses and consumers to engage in certain behaviours or make specific choices based on economic advantages. Marketing incentives can be highly motivational for individuals and businesses. They employ various types of influence, but they usually provide financial benefits such as tax credits and cash rebates. These financial rewards can strongly motivate individuals and businesses to adopt certain behaviours or make specific choices that align with the objectives of the incentive. In many cases, the marketing incentives reduce the overall cost of adopting sustainable or environmentally friendly practices (e.g., tax credits for renewable energy installations).

As a rule, marketing incentives are tied to compliance with regulations. Non-compliance may result in penalties or higher costs, which serves as a strong motivation for businesses to adhere to the prescribed practices. However, the effectiveness of marketing incentives can vary depending on factors like the size of the incentive, the clarity of the eligibility criteria and the perceived benefits. Additionally, some individuals and businesses may prioritise short-term financial gains over long-term sustainability, which can affect their responses to incentives.

Below are some examples of benefits that are offered by governments to ensure adoption of a circular economy and make clean energy more financially appealing (Delbeke & Vis, 2015):

- Many governments offer tax incentives to individuals and businesses that invest in renewable energy sources like solar panels and wind turbines;
- Some regions provide cash rebates or tax credits to individuals who purchase EVs;
- Feed-in tariffs for green energy that guarantee a fixed payment rate for electricity generated from renewable sources;
- Carbon pricing mechanisms like carbon taxes and cap-and-trade systems put a price on carbon emissions. This incentivises businesses to reduce their emissions to avoid higher costs, encouraging greener practices (Meadows et al., 2015);
- Deposit-return systems. In some places, consumers pay a deposit on beverage containers like bottles and cans. They receive a refund when they return the empty containers, promoting recycling and reducing waste. In Poland such a deposit system will be introduced at the beginning of 2025. Customers will be able to reclaim the deposit on returning the packaging (Wiński et al., 2023);
- Green building certification. Buildings that meet certain energy-efficiency and sustainability criteria, such as LEED (Leadership in Energy and Environmental Design) [https://www.usgbc.org/leed], can receive tax breaks or expedited permitting;
- Some governments provide subsidies to farmers who adopt sustainable farming practices, such as organic farming and conservation tillage;
- Research and development (R&D) tax credits. Businesses may receive tax credits for investing in R&D activities, which can incentivise innovation and development of new technologies;

- Tradeable pollution permits. Cap-and-trade systems allow businesses to buy and sell permits to emit a certain amount of pollutants. This encourages emission reduction by rewarding companies that emit less than their allocated limit;
- Consumer discounts for recycling. Some recycling programs offer discounts or coupons to consumers who recycle specific items such as electronics or old appliances at designated collection centres.

These marketing incentives are designed to align economic interests with environmental or societal goals, encouraging sustainable practices and responsible consumption. They can play a significant role in addressing environmental and social challenges while promoting economic growth.

Apart from financial and other marketing incentives, environmentally responsible enterprises may receive awards or certificates for innovative circular economy projects, products or initiatives. Certificates and rewards related to the circular economy can vary depending on the organisation or programme. Below are some examples:

- CEI certificates. The Circular Economy Institute [https://ceinstitute.org/] is a private training agency founded by Anna Tari. The institute provides continuing seminars, training, webcasts and publications to allow alumni and other stakeholders to stay up to date with developments in the circular economy. They offer a personalised up-to-date practical certification programme allowing participants to implement circularity with tools and advice from the world's top circular economy experts.
- Cradle-to-cradle certification. Products and companies can receive certification for their environmentally friendly design and material choices. The Cradle to Cradle Certified® Product Standard [https://c2ccertified.org/the-standard] provides a framework to assess the safety, circularity and responsibility of materials and products in five categories of sustainability performance: material health, product circularity, clean air and climate protection, water and soil stewardship, social fairness.
- ISO 14001 [https://www.iso.org/]. This Environmental Management System certification, while not specific to the circular economy, demonstrates a commitment to sustainability and environmental responsibility. It maps out a framework that a company or organisation can follow to set up an effective environmental management system. Designed for any type of organisation regardless of its activity or sector, it can provide assurance to company management, employees and external stakeholders that environmental impacts are being measured and improved (see also Jabbour et al., 2020).
- B Corp certification [https://www.bcorporation.net/en-us/certification/]. Companies that meet rigorous social and environmental standards can earn B Corp certification, which aligns with circular economy values. Unlike other certifications for businesses, B Lab is unique in its ability to measure a company's entire social and environmental impact.

- Sustainability Innovation Awards [https://sustainability-awards.me/] is one of the leading events applauding the achievements of Middle East sustainability initiatives and projects in all sectors. The awards strive to recognise individual excellence, corporate strengths and project success in all sectors. Companies are invited to nominate the people, projects and initiatives which they are most proud of.
- LIFE Awards [https://cinea.ec.europa.eu/programmes/life/best-projects-and-life-awards_en]. Every year the European Commission assess all completed LIFE projects and recognises the most innovative, inspirational and effective projects in three categories: nature protection, environment and climate action. The winners are selected by an expert jury and announced on the day of the ceremony, which takes place during the EU Green Week – Europe's biggest environmental event. Additionally, the LIFE Citizens' Prize allows the general public to get to know the finalists and vote for their preferred project online.
- Certification labels: Organisations like Fair Trade or the United States Department of Agriculture (Organic and Energy Star) use certification labels to help consumers identify sustainable and ethical products. These labels serve as marketing tools by signalling the sustainability credentials of products.

In Poland there are also organisations and institutions that have established rewards for sustainable behaviour, for example:

Business Associations. Industry-specific associations and chambers of commerce in Poland, such as the Polish Business and Innovation Centres Association (PBICA) [https://www.sooipp.org.pl/en], may offer awards or incentives to businesses that demonstrate a commitment to circular economy practices in their sectors.

Environmental NGOs. NGOs in Poland, like the Polish Ecological Club (Polski Klub Ekologiczny) and its regional branches [http://zgpke.pl/] organise awards and recognition programmes for individuals and organisations contributing to the circular economy and sustainability.

Business Competitions. Entrepreneurship and innovation competitions, such as the Polish edition of the European Social Innovation Competition, often include categories related to circular economy solutions. The Competition acts as a beacon for social innovators across Europe, incentivising and rewarding early-stage ideas and shaping society for the better [https://eic.ec.europa.eu/eic-prizes/european-social-innovation-competition_en].

These organisations and bodies play a crucial role in promoting and rewarding circular economy initiatives in Poland, encouraging businesses, entrepreneurs and individuals to adopt sustainable and circular practices. Therefore, such certificates and rewards contribute to the promotion and adoption of circular economy principles and practices, encouraging sustainability and responsible resource management.

Solving sustainability challenges is a complex task that requires collaboration and commitment by a wide range of stakeholders. Progress often comes from the combined efforts of governments, businesses, civil society and individuals working together towards a more sustainable future. Governments and international organisations are not only policymakers but may also motivate individuals and entrepreneurs to implement more sustainable activities with financial rewards or grants to support circular economy initiatives and research.

NGOs like Greenpeace, the World Wildlife Fund and The Nature Conservancy work to protect the environment, advocate sustainable practices and raise public awareness of critical sustainability issues.

Businesses have a significant impact on sustainability by adopting sustainability initiatives, reducing their carbon footprint and developing eco-friendly products and supply chain practices. Sustainable business practices can help drive positive change. Marketing activities in sustainability aim to align businesses with consumer values and preferences for eco-friendly and socially responsible products and practices. Influencers and celebrities who focus on sustainability and eco-conscious living can partner with brands to promote sustainable products or lifestyles to their followers. These efforts can drive positive change by encouraging sustainable consumption and production.

Education and research institutions empower individuals to advocate sustainable policies and practices at the local, national and global levels. Informed citizens can drive positive change through activism and voting.

The activities of sustainable stakeholders play a crucial role in promoting sustainability by raising awareness, influencing consumer behaviour and driving demand for sustainable products and practices.

## References


Anderson, A. (2011). Sources, media, and modes of climate change communication: The role of celebrities. *Wiley Interdisciplinary Reviews: Climate Change*, *2*(4), 535–546.

Baah, C., Afum, E., Agyabeng-Mensah, Y., & Agyeman, D. O. (2022). Stakeholder influence on adoption of circular economy principles: Measuring implications for satisfaction and green legitimacy. *Circular Economy and Sustainability*, *2*(1), 91–111. https://doi.org/10.1007/s43615-021-00093-2

Bitzer, V., & Glasbergen, P. (2015). BusinessNGO partnerships in global value chains: part of the solution or part of the problem of sustainable change? *Current Opinion in Environmental Sustainability*, *12*, 35–40.

Bryson, J. (1995). *Strategic Planning for Public and Non-profit Organizations*. San Francisco: Jossey-Bass Publishers.

Cai, Y. J., & Choi, T. M. (2019). Extended producer responsibility: A systematic review and innovative proposals for improving sustainability. *IEEE Transactions on Engineering Management*, *68*(1), 272–288.

Camacho-Otero, J., Boks, C., & Pettersen, I. N. (2018). Consumption in the circular economy: A literature review. *Sustainability*, *10*(8), 2758.

Delbeke, J., & Vis, P. (Eds.) (2015). *EU Climate Policy Explained*. European Union: Routledge.

Doni, F., Gasperini, A., & Torres Soares, J. (2020). *SDG13 – Climate Action: Combatting Climate Change and its Impacts*. Bingley: Emerald Publishing Limited.

Epperly, B., & Lee, T. (2015). Corruption and NGO sustainability: A panel study of post-communist states. *VOLUNTAS: International Journal of Voluntary and Nonprofit Organizations*, *26*, 171–197.

Ferasso, M., Beliaeva, T., Kraus, S., Clauss, T., & Ribeiro-Soriano, D. (2020). Circular economy business models: The state of research and avenues ahead. *Business Strategy and the Environment*, *29*(8), 3006–3024.

Francis, P. (2015). *Praise be to you: Laudato Si': On care for our common home*. San Francisco (CA): Ignatius Press.

Freeman, R. E. (1984). *Strategic Management: A Stakeholder Approach*. Massachusetts: Pitman.

Freeman, R. E., & Mcvea, J. (2001). Strategic management: A stakeholder approach, *SSRN Electronic Journal*, *1*(01-02), 1–32. https://doi.org/10.2139/ssrn.263511

Goodman, M., Doyle, J., & Farrell, N. (2017). Celebrities and climate change. In M. Nisbet (Ed.), *Oxford Research Encyclopedia of Climate Science*. Oxford: Oxford University Press USA.

Goyal, S., Chauhan, S., & Mishra, P. (2021). Circular economy research: A bibliometric analysis (2000–2019) and future research insights. *Journal of Cleaner Production*, *287*, 125011.

Green Production Guide (2016). The PGA Green Unified Best Practices Guide. Retrieved 26 May 2021, from https://www.greenproductionguide.com/wp-content/uploads/2016/05/2016_PGA-Green-Unified-Best-Practices-Guide.pdf

Hollo, T. (2014). *Key Change: The Role of the Creative Industries in Climate Change Action*. Australia: Australian National University, College of Law.

Ishaq, M. I., & Di Maria, E. (2020). Sustainability countenance in brand equity: A critical review and future research directions. *Journal of Brand Management*, *27*(1), 15–34.

Jabbour, C. J. C., Seuring, S., de Sousa Jabbour, A. B. L., Jugend, D., Fiorini, P. D. C., Latan, H., & Izeppi, W. C. (2020). Stakeholders, innovative business models for the circular economy and sustainable performance of firms in an emerging economy facing institutional voids. *Journal of Environmental Management*, *264*, 110416.

Jager, J., & O'Riordan, T. (Eds.) (2019). *The Politics of Climate Change: A European Perspective*. Abingdon: Routledge.

Liu, S. Y., Napier, E., Runfola, A., & Cavusgil, S. T. (2020). MNE-NGO partnerships for sustainability and social responsibility in the global fast-fashion industry: A loose-coupling perspective. *International Business Review*, *29*(5), 101736.

Lock, I., & Seele, P. (2017). Theorizing stakeholders of sustainability in the digital age. *Sustainability Science*, *12*, 235–245.

Lozano, R. (2009). *Orchestrating Organisational Change for Corporate Sustainability: Strategies to Overcome Resistance to Change and to Facilitate Institutionalization*. United Kingdom: Cardiff University.

Martinat, S., et al. (2016). Sustainable urban development in a city affected by heavy industry and mining? Case study of brownfields in Karvina, Czech Republic. *Journal of Cleaner Production*, *118*, 78–87.

McKenzie, B. (2008). The places of pedagogy: Or, what we can do with culture through intersubjective experiences. Environmental Education Research, *14*(3), 361–373.

Meadows, D., Slingenberg, Y., & Zapfel, P. (2015). EU ETS: Pricing carbon to drive cost-effective reductions across Europe. In J. Delbeke & P. Vis (Eds.), *EU Climate Policy Explained*. European Union: Routledge.

Mirońska, D. (2016). *Relacje z interesariuszami organizacji non profit z perspektywy marketingowej*. Warszawa: Oficyna Wydawnicza SGH.

Moser, S. C. (2016). Reflections on climate change communication research and practice in the second decade of the 21st century: What more is there to say? *Wiley Interdisciplinary Reviews: Climate Change*, *7*(3), 345–369.

Nikkhah, H. A., & Redzuan, M. R. B. (2010). The role of NGOs in promoting empowerment for sustainable community development. *Journal of Human Ecology*, *30*(2), 85–92.

PMBOK®. (2021). *A Guide to the Project Management Body of Knowledge. Seventh* Edition. Pennsylvania: Project Management Institute.

Poret, S. (2019). Corporate-NGO partnerships through sustainability labeling schemes: Motives and risks. *Sustainability*, *11*(9), 2689.

Pouikli, K. (2020). Concretising the role of extended producer responsibility in European union waste law and policy through the Lens of the circular economy. *ERA Forum*, *20*(4), 491–508.

Prymon-Ryś, E. (2015). Znaczenie zarządzania relacjami w fundraisingu organizacji non-profit. *Marketing i Rynek*, 508–519. http://bazekon.icm.edu.pl/bazekon/element/bwmeta1.element.ekon-element-000171403371

Rimmer, M. (2012). Sorting out the Green From the Greenwash. WME – Water, Materials, Energy – Environment Business Magazine (pp. 1). Retrieved 31 May 2021, from http://works.bepress.com/matthew_rimmer/110/

Ryś, A. (2015). Planowane postarzanie produktu – analiza zjawiska [Planned product obsolescence – Analysis of the phenomenon]. *Zeszyty Naukowe Wyższej Szkoły Humanitas. Zarządzanie z*, *1*, 121–128.

Ryś, A., & Prymon-Ryś, E., (2017). *Tworzenie wartości w przedsiębiorstwach produkcyjnych a zjawisko planowego postarzania produktu* [Creating value in manufacturing industry vs. planned product obsolescence]. *Handel Wewnętrzny: rynek, przedsiębiorstwo, konsumpcja, marketing: pismo środowiska badaczy problemów rynku*. R. 63 nr 5, pp. 327–335.

Silva, M. E., Sousa-Filho, J. M., de, Yamim, A. P., & Diógenes, A. P. (2020). Exploring nuances of green skepticism in different economies. *Marketing Intelligence and Planning*, *38*(4), 449–463. https://doi.org/10.1108/MIP-10-2018-0435

Song, J., Sun, Y., & Jin, L. (2017). PESTEL analysis of the development of the waste-to-energy incineration industry in China. *Renewable and Sustainable Energy Reviews*, *80*, 276–289.

Tait, B. (2020). *Relationship Management: The Key To Achieving It All*. Forbes, https://www.forbes.com/sites/forbescoachescouncil/2020/03/31/

Trocki, M., Bukłaha, E., Grucza, B., Juchniewicz, M., Metelski, W., & Wyrozębski, P. (2013). *Nowoczesne zarządzanie projektami*. Warszawa: PWE.

Unerman, J., & O'Dwyer, B. (2010). NGO accountability and sustainability issues in the changing global environment. *Public Management Review*, *12*(4), 475–486.

Vergura, D. T., Zerbini, C., Luceri, B., & Palladino, R. (2023). Investigating sustainable consumption behaviors: A bibliometric analysis. *British Food Journal*, *125*(13), 253–276. https://doi.org/10.1108/BFJ-06-2022-0491

Wessels, T. (2013). *The Myth of Progress: Toward a Sustainable Future*. Hanover and London: UPNE.

Wiernik, B. M., Ones, D. S., & Dilchert, S. (2013). Age and environmental sustainability: A meta-analysis. *Journal of Managerial Psychology*, *28*(7/8), 826–856.

Wiński, K., Pamuła, & Wyszyńska, W. (2023). *Projekt ustawy wprowadzającej system kaucyjny przyjęty przez rząd*. PwC Studio – Prawo i Podatki. Retrieved 20 September 2023, from https://studio.pwc.pl/aktualnosci/legislacja/projekt-ustawy-wprowadzajacej-system-kaucyjny

Wójcik-Karpacz, A. (2018). Implikacje praktyczne teorii interesariuszy: Czego mniejsze firmy mogą się nauczyć od większych względem interesariuszy wewnętrznych? *Studia Ekonomiczne*, *348*, 7–25. http://cejsh.icm.edu.pl/cejsh/element/bwmeta1.element.cejsh-d603d008-df1e-46b1-81b0-d8f88882d7ca

## Websites

350.org, https://350.org/about/

B Corp Certification, https://www.bcorporation.net/en-us/certification/

Circular Economy Institute, https://ceinstitute.org/

Conservation International, https://www.conservation.org/

Consumer Goods Forum (CGF), https://www.theconsumergoodsforum.com/

Cradle to Cradle Certified® Product Standard, https://c2ccertified.org/the-standard

Eco-Age, https://eco-age.com

European Social Innovation Competition, https://eic.ec.europa.eu/eic-prizes/european-social-innovation-competition_en

Fundacja "Ekopotencjał – Przestrzeń Możliwości, https://ekopotencjal.pl/

Fundacja Kupuj Odpowiedzialnie, https://ekonsument.pl/s56_what_we_do.html

Fundacja Nasza Ziemia, https://www.naszaziemia.pl/english/

Fundacja Zielony Ład, https://www.fundacjazielonylad.pl/

Good On You, https://goodonyou.eco/emma-watson-good-on-you-supporter/

Greenpeace foundation, https://www.greenpeace.org/poland/

Heated, https://heated.world/about

ICLEI, https://iclei.org/

Infuture Institute, https://infuture.institute/

Instytut Praw Obywatelskich, https://instytutsprawobywatelskich.pl/

ISO 14001, https://www.iso.org/

Jane Goodall Institute, https://janegoodall.org/

Koalicja Klimatyczna, https://koalicjaklimatyczna.org/o-nas

LEED, https://www.usgbc.org/leed

Leonardo DiCaprio Foundation, https://foundationguide.org/foundations/leonardo-dicaprio-foundation/

LIFE Awards, https://cinea.ec.europa.eu/programmes/life/best-projects-and-life-awards_en

Ministerstwo Klimatu i Środowiska, https://www.gov.pl/web/klimat

Nature Conservancy, https://www.nature.org/en-us/

Oleśnica: Miasto Zero Waste, https://olesnica.naszemiasto.pl/tag/zero-waste

Ośrodek Działań Ekologicznych 'Źródła', https://www.zrodla.org/english/

Oxfam International, https://www.oxfam.org/en

Polish Business and Innovation Centers Association (PBICA), https://www.sooipp.org.pl/en
Polski Klub Ekologiczny, http://zgpke.pl/
Polskie Stowarzyszenie Budownictwa Ekologicznego PLGBC, https://plgbc.org.pl/
Polskie Stowarzyszenie "Zero Waste", https://zero-waste.pl/o-nas/#nasza-misja
Prokarde, https://prokarde.org/
Rainforest Foundation, https://rainforestfoundation.org/about/mission-history/
SEI Foundation, https://www.sei.org/
Sierra Club, https://www.sierraclub.org/explore-issues
SolarAid, https://solar-aid.org/
Stowarzyszenie Ekologiczne EKO-UNIA, https://eko-unia.org.pl/en/
Sustainability Innovation Awards, https://sustainability-awards.me/
Sustsinability & Innovation Hub Evoqua, https://www.evoqua.com/en-150/
TriplePundit, https://www.triplepundit.com/
Wärtsilä's Sustainable Technology Hub (STH), https://www.sustainabletechnologyhub.com/
Water.org, https://water.org/about-us/
World Wide Fund for Nature, https://www.worldwildlife.org/

# 4 Examples of activities of enterprises in a circular economy

## 4.1 Methods: an overview of circular economy and sustainable marketing practices

The case study method involves a thorough examination of one or more cases in order to understand their contexts, processes and outcomes. It is a qualitative approach that allows analysis of real phenomena in their natural environment. The case study method is a key element in this study, and it has made it possible to learn and present specific examples of sustainable marketing activities and practices of companies in the context of a circular economy.

The data collected are defined as sets of initiatives taking place at a given time and place, over which the researcher has no control. According to Yin (2015, p. 36), this is the basic reason for the use of the case study method. Moreover, the specificity of doubts that have emerged, such as 'why?' and 'how?' questions as identified by Ćwiklicki and Urbaniak (2019, pp. 25–26), together with meeting an additional criterion, which is the need to study the phenomena in actually occurring conditions, confirmed the authors in the correctness of their choice of the case study method for this chapter. Following recommendations by researchers Yin (2015, pp. 96–100) and Ćwiklicki and Urbaniak (2019, pp. 35–56) and aiming for a broader understanding of the specificity of projects, it was decided to use the multiple case study method, which is identical to the approach of Creswell (2007, pp. 78–79) and which takes into account the operation of more than one unit in the analysis. Data were collected through observation, analysis of documents and online content, as well as in follow-up interviews with decision-makers in selected market facilities.

The case studies presented provide inspiration for other companies, showing that sustainable marketing and circular economy practices not only benefit the environment but also translate into business success. They show that it is possible to simultaneously make a profit and engage in social and ecological aims. Exploring these inspiring examples opens the door to a new era in marketing, the circular economy and responsible business in Poland. The examples are discussed chronologically from the oldest to the newest in order to observe possible trends. Have circular economy and sustainable marketing

DOI: 10.4324/9781003408642-5

practices significantly advanced in the last five years? In which areas? What developments of the phenomenon and its popularity among enterprises in Poland can be further predicted? Answers to these and other key questions are provided in Section 4.2 and the conclusions in Section 4.3.

## 4.2 An overview of circular economy and sustainable marketing practices

In order to present the most up-to-date practices related to the circular economy and sustainable marketing, it was decided to conduct a review covering a five-year period (2018–2022), which consists of 55 practices (case studies) (2018 – 5 practices, 2019 – 16 internships, 2020 – 14 internships, 2021 – 14 internships, 2022 – 6 internships). Examples of enterprises covering a wide range of different industries (including construction, finance, trade, wood, paper and furniture, clothing and services) were selected showing the variety of possibilities of the application of these practices.

**Practice: Environmentally friendly packaging**
**Company: Henkel Polska**
**Industry: FMCG, Chemicals**
**Year: 2018**

In 2018, Henkel set new aims that support the circular economy. By 2025, the company aims to make 100% of its product packaging environmentally friendly, meaning that it can be recycled, reused or composted. Additionally, Henkel plans that by 2025, 35% of the plastic product packaging it produces in Europe will be produced from plastic waste. A new cosmetics brand was launched on the market, the bottles for which are made of 25% recycled plastic materials. In addition, its adhesive packaging is now 100% recyclable (Henkel Polska, 2019).

Henkel actively takes action to reduce its impact on the environment and to promote sustainable solutions in packaging production.

**Practice: Report on the circular economy**
**Company: ING Bank Śląski**
**Industry: Finance**
**Year: 2018**

ING Bank Śląski was a strategic partner in a Deloitte report entitled 'Closed circulation – open opportunities' on the circular economy. The report was presented at the EEC (European Economic Congress) Green conference, an event accompanying COP24 in Katowice. The aim of the document was to look at the situation in Poland and identify opportunities created by the circular economy. It was the first study of this type on the Polish market that presented an economic analysis of the phenomenon, and it included indicators of the economic benefits for Poland (ING Bank Śląski, 2019).

In sustainable marketing, the main aim is not only to promote products and services but also to engage in education, research and sustainable development practices. ING Bank Śląski's partnership in developing the report on the circular economy is an example of such an approach that contributes to increasing awareness and promoting sustainable practices.

**Practice: Siekierki Ash Separation Plant**
**Company: Lafarge**
**Industry: Construction and real estate**
**Year: 2018**

As part of cooperation between Lafarge and PGNiG Termika, the Siekierki Ash Separation Plant (ZSPS) was established. The plant cleans fly ash produced during coal combustion and transforms it into two types of products that are put back into circulation. The investment implements the assumptions of the circular economy. The resulting ProAsh® and High Carbon fuel are used in various segments of the economy including industry and the construction sector (Lafarge, 2019).

The cooperation between two large companies, Lafarge and PGNiG Termika, to implement the project is an example of a sustainable business partnership that can influence the positive image and reputation of both companies. The initiative can be treated as a marketing strategy that involves introducing innovative products or solutions to the market that are sustainable and bring environmental benefits.

**Practice: Reduction of water use**
**Company: L'Oréal Polska**
**Industries: Pharmaceuticals, FMCG, Chemicals**
**Year: 2018**

As part of its 'Sharing Beauty with All' project, L'Oréal Polska committed to reduce water consumption by 60%. The L'Oréal Warsaw Plant made investments such as in installing new flow meters, developing a water consumption map, implementing a steam cleaning process and creating cooling system production platforms in a closed loop. Each new modification of the production process and change in the factory was assessed for its impact on the environment, especially in terms of water consumption. Thanks to the innovations introduced, by the end of 2018 compared to 2005 water consumption was reduced by 42%, while production increased by 250% (L'Oréal Polska, 2019).

Sustainable marketing practices such as those of L'Oréal Polska include defining sustainable goals, investing in sustainable technologies, assessing impacts on the environment and consistently striving to reduce water consumption and increase production, while taking care of ecology.

**Practice: Packaging strategy**
**Company: Carrefour Polska**

**Industry: Trade**
**Year: 2018**

Carrefour's packaging strategy specifies the commitments the chain has made to reduce the weight of packaging and optimise it. The company committed to support the circular economy model by promoting packaging that is more environmentally friendly. The main aims of Carrefour Polska were to reduce the weight of its own brand packaging by 5% by 2022 compared to 2017 and to introduce 100% recyclable or compostable own brand packaging by 2025 (Carrefour Polska, 2019).

Carrefour has implemented a packaging strategy that aims to reduce the company's impact on the environment and promote environmentally friendly packaging. It is taking concrete steps to achieve its sustainability goals, such as reducing the weight of its own brand packaging and introducing recyclable and compostable packaging. It is also striving to reduce raw material consumption and waste through more efficient use of packaging. Promoting environmentally friendly packaging aims to attract customers who are increasingly aware of ecological problems and contributes to a positive image of the company.

**Practice: An eco-solution in a catalyst factory in Środa Śląska**
**Company: BASF Polska**
**Industry: Chemicals**
**Year: 2019**

BASF introduced an environmental solution in its catalytic converter factory in Środa Śląska by replacing disposable plastic cups with its biodegradable ecovio® plastic cups. Biodegradable ecovio® cups are deposited in dedicated waste bins equipped with biodegradable ecovio® bags. The cups then go to a biocomposter, into which employees also put organic waste such as meal leftovers. After several weeks of composting, fertiliser is produced and it is used to fertilise the bee meadow on the factory premises, which supports the biodiversity of pollinating insects. The biocomposter is located in the office building, in the kitchenette, and does not emit unpleasant odours. Thanks to the introduction of biodegradable ecovio® cups and the composter, over five hundred plastic cups a day do not end up in landfills (BASF Polska, 2020).

The BASF initiative combines several elements of sustainable marketing. The introduction of biodegradable cups shows the company's concern for the natural environment, reduces the amount of plastic waste and promotes the use of more ecological materials. Additionally, supporting biodiversity by fertilising the bee meadow emphasises its commitment to environmental protection. The company provides transparent information about the biocomposting process, which builds its image as an organisation that cares about the comfort of its employees. This practice is part of the global trend of plastic reduction and contributes to reducing landfill waste, which is consistent with a sustainable approach. As a result, it is an example of sustainable marketing that combines business aims with concern for the natural environment, waste reduction and the promotion of ecological alternatives.

**Practice: ZERO water waste**
**Company: Carlsberg Polska**
**Industry: FMCG**
**Year: 2019**

Carlsberg Polska carried out a 'ZERO water waste' programme, which aimed to reduce water consumption in breweries. By monitoring and optimising processes, the company achieved savings by reducing water consumption in beer production. The programme included water reclamation, recycling and water quality monitoring using fish as indicators. The ultimate aim was to significantly reduce water consumption in the brewing industry (Carlsberg, 2020).

This programme not only contributed to the achievement of sustainable development and environmental protection aims but also allowed Carlsberg Polska to build a positive company image and attract customers who value a sustainable ecological approach.

**Practice: Public DIY 'Men's Shed' workshops**
**Company: Jula Poland**
**Industry: Trade**
**Year: 2019**

The 'Men's Shed' project was an initiative implemented by Jula Poland in cooperation with the Nasza Ziemia Foundation and local partners. It involved creating public DIY workshops in which anyone could repair and refurbish things that would otherwise be thrown away free of charge. The Jula chain sponsored equipment and tools for these workshops, which were especially targeted at seniors over 65 years of age, although access to the workshops was open to everyone (Jula, 2020).

The 'Men's Shed' workshops enjoyed great interest among local communities, which contributed to their integration and activation. Residents could implement individual projects but the workshops also became places enabling cooperation on joint projects involving and integrating various groups. As a result, the 'Męska Szopa' project became a long-term commitment of the company and its partners to promote a sustainable approach to consumption and the integration of local communities. This continued as part of the following events: 'Mikołajkowa Zawierucha' – intergenerational DIY in Warsaw; and 'Szopa z Klasą' –workshops to construct furniture made of pallets for students at the nearby Primary School No. 66 in Warsaw and classes in making wooden bears for students at Primary School No. 6 in Słupsk.

**Practice: Heat recovery from industrial processes for district heating**
**Company: Veolia**

**Industry: Energy, Recycling**
**Year: 2019**

Veolia Energia Poznań, part of the Veolia Group in Poland, in cooperation with the Volkswagen Poznań Foundry implemented a solution for recovering heat from industrial processes for district heating. In this project, heat emitted by compressors in an industrial plant, which generated huge amounts of heat during the compression process, was effectively recovered and used. The annual savings amounted to as much as 17 million litres of water and almost 40,000 GJ of energy, which meant a total reduction in carbon dioxide emissions of over 5,000 tons. The heat recovered from the compression process was transmitted to 30 nearby buildings, including a hospital, which ensured efficient use of this energy (Veolia, 2020).

Veolia Energia Poznań and Odlewnia Volkswagen Poznań established a partnership that enables effective heat recovery from industrial processes, constituting one of the first such solutions in Central and Eastern Europe. This initiative not only brings real ecological benefits but also has a positive impact on the local community. This is a clear example of how a sustainable approach by industry can benefit both the environment and the local community at the same time.

**Practice: Using waste gas to produce heat**
**Company: Veolia Group**
**Industry: Energy, Recycling**
**Year: 2019**

Veolia Group in Poland in cooperation with the Miasteczko Śląskie Commune carried out a project to use waste gas to produce heat. A zinc smelter located in the Miasteczko Śląskie commune produced low-energy gas as a by-product, which had been a problem for the plant and the environment. Following the changes, the heat obtained by burning this gas is distributed using pump systems to buildings in the city through a low-temperature heating network. The heating plant burns 6.3 million cubic metres of waste gas from the zinc production process, which allows over 60,000 GJ of heat to be obtained annually, which Veolia supplies to the city's inhabitants and to the steelworks itself (Veolia Group, 2020).

The Veolia Group project involves using waste gas to produce heat, minimising waste and making efficient use of available resources; cooperation with local authorities, which indicates the company's commitment to developing sustainable solutions in cooperation with local communities; effective distribution of heat to buildings in the city, improving energy efficiency and using renewable energy sources; and reducing environmental problems by converting waste gas into useful heat, which helps to solve problems for both the environment and the plant and sends a positive message to customers and the local community. The project promotes sustainable development, care for the natural environment and efficient use of resources, which are important aspects of sustainable marketing.

**Practice: Anwiloteka**
**Company: ANWIL**
**Industry: Chemicals**
**Year: 2019**

The Anwilotek project introduced by ANWIL consisted of a simple book exchange system in which the company's employees brought volumes they had read to share them with others and exchange them for other books. The library was completely voluntary and trusted with no library cards or people serving readers. The main rule was simple: take a book, read it and return it to its place. The collection was supplemented in a similar way so everyone could share their book with others by leaving it on a shelf. Anwiloteka aimed not only to promote reading among the company's employees but also to draw attention to the circular economy as an important aspect of everyday life (Anwil, 2020).

The sustainable marketing activities in the ANWIL Anwiloteka project include promoting book exchanging, an absence of formalities and library cards, education and promotion of reading, together with emphasising the importance of the circular economy. The project aimed not only to promote reading but also to emphasise the importance of engaging in sustainable practices such as exchanging, reusing and reducing resources and education about a sustainable lifestyle, which is important in the context of sustainable marketing.

**Practice: B2B2C online upcycling platform**
**Company: Deko Eko**
**Industry: Services**
**Year: 2019**

Deko Eko has implemented a B2B2C online platform bringing together three important user groups: companies generating waste, creators specialising in upcycling and consumers. The aim of this platform is to accelerate and automate trade-related processes and connect by means of a so-called smart matching mechanism company with innovative ideas with companies that actively seek to use their waste efficiently. As a result of this ecosystem, waste that is difficult to process is transformed into valuable products, giving it new value, solving problems related to waste disposal and generating new opportunities to generate profits. Business customers can register their accounts on the Dekoeko.com platform, which gives them the opportunity to order a prototype of a selected product made from their own waste, purchase more products and make their waste available to other designers for processing purposes. In the first few months of operation, the platform managed to attract as many as 211 clients and designers specialising in upcycling. The platform presented 173 unique products in over 20 different categories using many types of waste raw materials, such as advertising banners, mesh nets, paper, plastic, PET (polyethylene terephthalate) bottles, electronic waste, catalogues and wood (Forum Odpowiedzialnego Biznesu, 2020).

The Deko Eko platform combines business innovation with care for the environment, which is an example of sustainable marketing that promotes ecological and effective reuse of materials. Additionally, there has been development of an ecosystem with upcycling designers and clients, which supports a community interested in sustainable solutions.

**Practice: Second life**
**Company: MindBlowing**
**Industry: Services**
**Year: 2019**

Instead of throwing away seemingly unnecessary promotional merchandise – in this case, banners and roll-up stands left over from conferences – MindBlowing and the Nielada Historia foundation decided to give a second life to these materials. The above-mentioned banners were used to make pouches for documents and airline tickets. In addition to their functionality, they had an original aesthetic appearance, thanks to which their users were happy to keep them for long-term use. Luggage tags produced using the same technique, designed so that they could be used as attractive business card holders, were also very popular (MindBlowing, 2020).

This initiative not only reduced waste but also encouraged customers to use these materials in the long term, reflecting sustainable values and promoting conscientious resource management.

**Practice: FoundGorzów**
**Company: Eneris**
**Industry: Raw materials and fuels**
**Year: 2019**

Eneris Environmental Protection joined forces with the social initiative Gorzów To My and Gorzów prison to carry out the 'FoundGorzów' campaign to give new life to used bicycles. A collection of old or broken folding bikes, highlanders, racing bikes, ladies' bikes and children's bikes was announced. Over 150 of them were gathered in a hall provided by the company. They were repaired and renovated by prisoners in the Gorzów Penitentiary as part of their socialisation and learning a new profession. After renovation, the bikes were given to needy families and children or lent to the residents of Gorzów as 'free city bikes' (Eneris, 2020).

The initiative promoted a balance between economic, social and environmental interests, which is characteristic of sustainable marketing. This contributed to improving the quality of life of the community and reducing the impact on the environment, which is a key element in sustainable development.

**Practice: Longer sofa life**
**Company: IKEA Retail**

**Industry: Wood, paper and furniture**
**Year: 2019**

IKEA Retail in Warsaw has implemented a test collection service for old sofas and armchairs in cooperation with the Habitat for Humanity Poland Foundation. IKEA customers who purchase a new sofa or armchair have the opportunity to donate their unnecessary furniture to the foundation. With the help of a transport company, IKEA delivers this furniture to the foundation, which uses it in social and aid programmes and which plans to open a charity shop in Warsaw where the furniture can be made available again (IKEA, 2020).

In this initiative, IKEA Retail implements several sustainable marketing practices: encouraging customers to donate used furniture; promoting its re-use instead of getting rid of it; highlighting involvement in social projects and helping those in need; and eliminating the need to produce new furniture, thereby reducing negative impacts on the environment. These sustainable marketing efforts promote both social and environmental aims while engaging customers in the SDGs.

**Practice: I'm not a hamster – I don't hamster**
**Company: European Leasing Fund**
**Industry: Finance**
**Year: 2019**

On the occasion of a change of headquarters, the European Leasing Fund carried out a campaign entitled 'I am not a hamster – I don't hamster'. A review of office equipment and supplies was made looking for things that the company had in excess and could share with those in need and other institutions. As a result, among other things, over 5,000 document sleeves, over 500 binders, over 300 document trays, over 100-hole punches, paper clips and other office supplies, furniture sets and computers were selected (Forum Odpowiedzialnego Biznesu, 2020).

The campaign was aimed at promoting sustainable marketing by minimising waste, educating employees on conscientious ownership and promoting the zero-waste philosophy. Cooperation with other institutions and pro-social activities were important elements in the campaign.

**Practice: Zero Waste Removals**
**Company: Intive**
**Industry: IT**
**Year: 2019**

Intive combined its two offices in Wrocław applying the zero-waste moving principle. Existing furniture was reused, being given to employees, local entities such as schools, foundations, non-governmental organisations, the company that rented part of the office space after Intive and to a company specialising in corporate furniture. This was supported by a furniture booking app created by Intive, which included an inventory of the items available. As a result of the move, over 80% of the furniture found new owners in the first stage and 68% in the second stage, which constitutes almost 75% of all the furniture available in the application. Employees had the opportunity to purchase these items, which allowed them to furnish their apartments in a favourable manner. The proceeds from the sale of furniture were allocated to a tree planting campaign supported by the Development Foundation/Dotlenieni.org, which resulted in the planting of 5,000 tree seedlings by the Intive branch in Wrocław (Intive, 2020).

As part of its sustainable marketing practices, the company donated furniture to foundations. However, this was only part of its commitment. Special cooperation was established with one of the schools outside Wrocław, which received new equipment, including desks, containers and chairs. This initiative not only supported student education and comfort but also contributed to the sustainable development of society. Moreover, the company decided to use the revenue from the sale of furniture in a sustainable way. This revenue was used to equip the new Intive office using environmentally friendly solutions. This is a perfect example of an approach that combines business benefits with pro-ecological activities. By investing in environmentally friendly solutions, the company promoted its commitment to protecting the planet while benefiting from business efficiency.

**Practice: Billboard on your back**
**Company: ING Bank Śląski**
**Industry: Finance**
**Year: 2019**

As part of its Billboard on Your Back campaign, ING Bank Śląski transformed outdoor advertisements into shopping bags, backpacks, waist bags and laptop cases. In this campaign, 4,700 $m^2$ of billboards were replaced with 7,400 ecological bags, backpacks, waist bags and laptop cases. In addition, branding banners, for example, after a football tournament, were transformed into backpacks for football players, who received them at subsequent sporting events. Bags, backpacks, waist bags and laptop cases also served as gifts for customers and employees in various competitions promoting the ideas of recycling and upcycling (ING Bank Śląski, 2020).

ING Bank Śląski's initiative supported sustainable marketing practices through recycling and upcycling, minimising waste, promoting recycling, providing ecological gifts to customers and employees and supporting sports initiatives. This underlined the bank's commitment to sustainable practices that care for the natural environment and promote efficient use of resources.

**Practice: Reusable boxes for a closed-loop economy**
**Company: Kaufland Polska Markety**
**Industry: Trade**
**Year: 2019**

In cooperation with Euro Pool System, Kaufland Polska Markety introduced reusable closed-circuit boxes. The EPS boxes were reusable, collapsible and fully recyclable. The service life of these boxes was on average seven years, during which they could be used many times. Since their introduction in Poland, these boxes have been used over 61 million times, which has translated into savings of significant amounts of cardboard and single-use plastic packaging. The use of these boxes contributed to a reduction of $CO_2$ emissions by Kaufland Polska. The ability to fold these boxes also helped to significantly reduce transport and storage needs. The use of EPS boxes also helped to avoid damage to goods, which resulted in less food waste. In addition, the introduction of these boxes saved raw materials that would otherwise have been used to produce less durable packaging, such as plastic, cardboard and wood, which were typically used once (Kaufland Polska Markety, 2020).

This practice combines social, ecological and economic factors, which is characteristic of sustainable marketing which seeks to achieve a balance between business profits and positive impacts on society and the environment. An additional educational aspect of the practice involved informing customers about the benefits of using durable, reusable packaging, which aimed to change consumer behaviour towards using more ecological packaging.

**Practice: Reuse service**
**Company: Stena Recycling**
**Industry: Recycling**
**Year: 2019**

Stena Recycling introduced a reuse service, which enabled reuse of LCD (Liquid Crystal Display) panels. This process took place at the Stena Recycling electronics recycling centre. After the devices arrived at the plant and a thorough technical inspection of the monitors, the undamaged panels were dismantled and sent to a cooperating TV manufacturer in Asia. The Asian manufacturer could use the working monitors to put new TVs on the market at affordable prices. In total, 600 tons of panels were recovered yearly (Forum Odpowiedzialnego Biznesu, 2020).

This initiative is consistent with sustainable marketing practices that promote environmental protection, waste minimisation, efficient use of resources and creation of additional value for companies and communities. It contributed to reducing electronic waste, which is important from both an ecological and a marketing point of view, promoting the company as environmentally responsible and sustainable.

**Practice: Cleaning, renovation and shoemaking services**
**Company: WoshWosh**
**Industry: Services**
**Year: 2019**

WoshWosh, which provides cleaning, renovation and shoemaking services, responded to the problem of excessive consumerism leading to overproduction of shoes. The company's aim is to make the public aware of how shoes are produced and how important it is to only choose ones that are well-made and the production of which do not harm anyone. Additionally, it shows how to care for shoes and how to pay attention to the environmental footprint we make when buying another pair. The company conducts many training courses and workshops, some of which are free of charge. Additionally, it organises shoe collections for the homeless, refurbishing, disinfecting and giving shoes to people in need (Wosh Wosh, 2020).

The sustainable marketing practices that WoshWosh implements include: creating awareness of excessive consumerism and overproduction of shoes; promoting sustainable purchasing choices; consumer education through training and workshops; social activities such as collecting shoes for the homeless and renovating them; and minimising waste by repairing and refurbishing shoes. These initiatives are part of the company's sustainable marketing policy, which not only promotes products but also strives to change consumer behaviour and contribute to the good of the community.

**Practice: Supporting the circular economy**
**Company: Ceetrus Polska**
**Industry: Construction and real estate**
**Year: 2020**

In each of the 24 commercial facilities belonging to Ceetrus Polska, customers can use service points that enable repairing of shoes, mobile phones and electronic equipment. In this way, the company tries to support the circular economy. Moreover, in front of most commercial facilities belonging to Ceetrus Polska, you can find bicycle shelters and self-service stations for vehicle repairs (Dobre praktyki CSR w Polsce, 2023).

Ceetrus Polska implements sustainable marketing by providing services that support the circular economy, promote sustainable transport and educate customers about a sustainable lifestyle. This contributes to building a positive brand image and introduces added value for customers by caring for the environment and encouraging responsible consumer choices.

**Internship: Circular economy at ING**
**Company: ING Bank Śląski**
**Industry: Finance**
**Year: 2020**

ING Bank Śląski takes initiatives and uses technological solutions consistent with the principles of a circular economy, such as the use of rainwater to water the greenery around the buildings of the ING Headquarters in Katowice and recovery of grey water for reuse in the ING facility in Ruda Śląska. Additionally, as part of the circular economy activities at ING, a platform has been created for the sale of furniture (desks, chairs and cabinets) from liquidations, relocations and modernisations. Each employee has the option to repurchase at an attractive price (ING Bank Śląski, 2021).

ING Bank Śląski undertakes sustainable marketing activities that promote the principles of the circular economy, minimise resource consumption and care for the natural environment. These initiatives not only contribute to sustainable development but also build a positive brand image and can influence employee involvement in pro-ecological activities.

**Practice: Żabka Polska implements a circular economy**
**Company: Żabka Polska**
**Industry: Trade**
**Year: 2020**

Żabka Polska is introducing a circular economy system, encouraging customers and franchisees to collect plastic bottles. The initiative is currently in the pilot phase and it is implemented in 23 shops in Warsaw. The packaging collected will be used to create bottles of OD NOWA mineral water. Żabka's aim is to create a habit in customers to return plastic beverage containers to shops, as is the case with glass bottles. Additionally, Żabka Polska and Żywiec Zdrój have established a strategic partnership and signed a letter of intent in which they committed to joint activities to reduce the use of plastics. Both companies have started testing EKOmats – special machines that enable selective collection of plastic and metal beverage containers. The first such devices were installed in 2020 in selected Żabka shops in Poznań and Warsaw, and the raw materials collected will be used to produce new bottles (Żabka, 2021).

Żabka Polska implements sustainable marketing by introducing initiatives in the fields of the circular economy, recycling and strategic partnerships. These initiatives not only help protect the environment but can also build a positive brand image and encourage customers to make more sustainable consumer choices.

**Practice: Smartphone regeneration**
**Company: T-Mobile Polska**
**Industry: Telecommunications**
**Year: 2020**

T-Mobile Polska launched a 'Smartphone regeneration' offer, in which phones were given a second life. For a symbolic one zloty, customers could purchase refurbished iPhones covered by a two-year warranty. Customers were offered alternatives to new frequently changed phone models, limiting the overconsumption of electronic equipment (T-Mobile Polska, 2022).

T-Mobile Polska promotes sustainable marketing by offering refurbished phones with a long warranty and encouraging customers to make more sustainable purchasing choices, which helps to reduce negative impacts on the environment (T-Mobile Polska, 2021).

**Practice: Second life – upcycling products**
**Company: Sopot Insurance Company ERGO Hestia**
**Industry: Finance**
**Year: 2020**

The 'Second Life – Upcycling Products' project is an initiative of the Sopot Insurance Company ERGO Hestia which involves processing waste through upcycling and creating various items from them, such as jewellery, fabric smartphone cases, promotional merchandise, competition prizes and even furniture that are used at the company's headquarters, for example, tables made from car wheels after accidents. As part of this project, ERGO Hestia cooperates with companies specialising in upcycling, such as Deko Eko, start-ups and designers who create products from waste. The company has also established cooperation with organisations dealing with recycling, segregation and preparation of waste for reuse. For this initiative, ERGO Hestia received a distinction in the Stena Circular Economy Award competition. Additionally, the company organised upcycling workshops for its employees as part of the 'Environmental Open Day' event. The effectiveness of the project is measured with various indicators such as the percentage of waste recycled or upcycled and the total funds allocated to upcycled or other consumable products. In 2019, 45% of the waste generated at ERGO Hestia was recycled or upcycled (ERGO Hestia, 2021).

ERGO Hestia promotes sustainable marketing through active involvement in upcycling, cooperation with various entities, employee education and monitoring the results of activities, which contributes to reducing waste, promoting sustainable resource management and creating a more environmentally friendly corporate culture.

**Practice: Old to new**
**Company: Auchan Retail Polska**
**Industry: Trade**
**Year: 2020**

As part of the annual 'Back to School' campaign, Auchan Retail Polska carried out a project related to the circular economy called 'Old to New'. In this initiative, a collection of old backpacks was organised in cooperation with the Eko Textil foundation, an expert in textile recycling. Every customer who brought an old backpack received a 50% discount on the purchase of a new backpack. As part of this campaign, a total of 6.35 tons of old backpacks were collected. All the backpacks were 100% recycled or reused, and the funds collected were used to purchase five tricycles for disabled children. A continuation of this initiative is planned (Auchan Retail Polska, 2022).

The 'Old to New' initiative by Auchan Retail Polska is an example of sustainable marketing that combines aspects of environmental protection, conscientious shopping and support for charities, while promoting the company's long-term commitment to these practices.

**Practice: Circular Economy Portal in practice**
**Company: CSR Consulting**
**Industry: Consulting**
**Year: 2020**

In 2020, a new portal called 'GOZ w praktyce' (CE in practice) was created, which was initiated by CSR Consulting and established business partnerships with BASF, Carlsberg Polska, Rekopol Packaging Recovery Organisation and Stena Recycling. This portal is a centre of knowledge and practical solutions in the area of the circular economy, and its aim is to support companies in the transformation process towards the EU model of the circular economy. It involves various tools and business solutions, including business models based on the principles of circularity, circular economy indicators and an overview of current legal regulations in Poland and the EU. The knowledge base includes dozens of examples of successful company practices, expert analyses, reports from Poland and abroad and the possibility to add one's own initiatives. The portal also hosts a virtual Circular Economy Academy. This project will be continually developed with the aim of creating a place for the exchange of ideas and joint development of the best circular solutions in the Polish market (Dobre praktyki CSR w Polsce, 2023).

The 'Circular Economy in Practice' portal is an example of sustainable marketing that promotes and supports the transformation towards a circular economy, providing knowledge, tools and inspiration for companies to take more sustainable actions.

**Practice: Activities of the Tubądzin Group to control water consumption**
**Company: Grupa Tubądzin**
**Industry: Trade**
**Year: 2020**

The Tubądzin Group focuses on the controlled use of water resources in its production activities, especially in the production of ceramic tiles. At the Ceramika Tubądzin III factory in Sieradz, a closed water circulation system was installed and its own sewage treatment plants were built. The process of polishing ceramic tiles requires the use of water, which is why the Tubądzin Group strives to ensure that the process is performed in an environmentally friendly manner and with respect for natural resources. With the launch of a modern polishing line at the end of 2019, the company built an ecological water treatment plant. This treatment plant is capable of filtering and purifying as much as 500 $m^3$ of water an hour. In 2020, the company used the full capacity of the sewage treatment plant throughout the year (Forum Odpowiedzialnego Biznesu, 2021).

The Tubądzin Group undertakes a number of practices related to the controlled use of water resources and environmental protection in the production process of ceramic tiles. These practices are examples of sustainable marketing that promotes a responsible approach to the management of natural resources.

**Practice: Cleaning and disinfection of work shoes**
**Company: WoshWosh**
**Industry: Services**
**Year: 2020**

In accordance with applicable regulations, work and employee footwear must be cleaned and disinfected even after a single use by an employee. Before 2018, no company offered such services, which led to the disposal of used shoes. However, since 2018 WoshWosh has introduced cleaning and disinfection services for work and employee footwear which allow it to be used longer and gives it a 'second life'. Thanks to this, the company achieved efficiency by reducing the amount of waste generated and cleaning and disinfecting approximately 9,000 pairs of work shoes (Dobre praktyki CSR w Polsce, 2023).

WoshWosh's initiatives related to the cleaning and disinfection of work and employee footwear are examples of sustainable marketing that contributes to environmental protection, waste reduction and efficient use of resources.

**Practice: Donating clothes**
**Company: Allianz Polska Group**
**Industry: Finance**
**Year: 2020**

Allianz Polska initiated a programme encouraging its employees to bring new or used but good quality undamaged and clean women's, men's and children's clothes (including jackets, blouses, trousers, dresses, shoes and accessories) to the office. There, the clothing was sorted and sent for reuse via the UbranieDoOddania.pl platform. Following the previous year's success, the company decided to expand this initiative by collecting clothes not only at its headquarters but also in five buildings managed by Colliers International Polska, including Platinium Business Park in Warsaw. The aim of the campaign was to support Allianz's long-time partner, SOS Children's Villages, with each 1 kg of clothing collected translated into PLN 1, which was used to cover the costs of medical visits and the purchase of necessary medicines for the association's patients. During the second edition of the 'Clothes to donate' campaign, 1,290.85 kg of clothing was collected, including one tonne donated by Allianz employees. This was twice as much as in the previous year. Thanks to the involvement of employees, they managed to donate PLN 1,024.79 to the SOS Children's Villages Association. The 'Clothes to donate' campaign involved collecting unused clothes lying in wardrobes. For each kilogram of good quality undamaged and clean clothing, PLN 1 was donated to cover monthly medical expenses for the children of SOS Children's Villages. As part of the initiative, employees could also learn what steps to take to become more conscientious customers of clothing stores. Thanks to this campaign, over a ton of clothes received a second life and did not end up in landfills (Forum Odpowiedzialnego Biznesu, 2021).

Allianz Polska's activities related to the 'Clothes to Donate' programme are examples of sustainable marketing that combines social and ecological factors and employee involvement, contributing to creating a positive impact on the community and the environment.

**Practice: Helping with clothes**
**Company: InterKadra**
**Industry: Services**
**Year: 2020**

Interkadra took part in a 'Helping through clothes' initiative, which involved ordering a container for the company's headquarters to collect unnecessary clothing, shoes, and so on, and sending information to the institution collecting clothes when it is full so that a new empty container is substituted. Each kilogram collected is worth a zloty, which the company donates to the 'Heart for a Maluszka' foundation (Dobre praktyki CSR w Polsce, 2023).

Interkadra's practices related to the 'Helping through Clothes' initiative are examples of sustainable marketing that integrates ecological and social goals, contributing to creating a positive impact on the environment and the community.

**Practice: Giving computers a second life**
**Company: Urtica**
**Industry: Pharmaceuticals**
**Year: 2020**

The 'We give computers a second life' campaign was an initiative of the Urtica Children Foundation which involved donating used computer equipment to children's oncology and haematology departments in Poland. The computers were serviced, given the necessary software and sent to hospitals to serve young patients and staff. The aim was not only to provide material assistance but also to enable children to contact their families and peers, especially during the pandemic. The campaign was successful, with 35 computer kits delivered to 5 hospitals, and the Foundation has plans to continue (Urtica, 2021).

To sum up, the 'We give computers a second life' campaign combines business aims, such as reusing used equipment, with social goals, that is, supporting children's oncology hospitals, which is an example of successful sustainable marketing. It advocates for the community and plans for a long-term impact on society and the environment.

**Practice: Collecting used footwear in stationary shops**
**Company: CCC Group**
**Industry: Trade**
**Year: 2020**

CCC carried out a 'Give your shoes a second life' campaign, in which it collected used shoes in its shops in Poland. The footwear collected was checked to see if it could be recovered and reused. The customers who brought used shoes received discount vouchers for purchases at CCC. The campaign aimed to promote shoe recycling and caring for the natural environment, in line with the company's sustainable development strategy. In the first three weeks of the campaign, over a ton of footwear was collected. The programme was active in 21 cities in Poland (CCC Group, 2021).

The campaign carried out by CCC is an example of sustainable marketing integrating business aims with care for the natural environment and society. The main elements of this practice are as follows: collection of used footwear – CCC organised the collection of used footwear in its shops in Poland, which aims to prevent and reduce waste by reusing and recycling footwear; recoverability analysis – before recycling or reusing, the footwear is checked to find optimal ways of recycling it; customer involvement – customers are asked to donate used shoes in special containers and they receive discount vouchers, which encourages them to participate in the campaign; programme expansion – the campaign is gradually expanding to more cities, demonstrating the company's commitment to sustainable practices on a larger scale; cooperation with the WoshWosh foundation – CCC cooperates with social organisations, donating the shoes collected to homeless people, which is a social aspect of sustainable marketing; a sustainable development strategy – this campaign is part of the CCC sustainable development strategy, which includes aims related to the concept of closed product circulation; customer awareness – the campaign promotes the idea of 'zero-waste' and emphasises the importance of caring for the natural environment, which helps build a positive image of the company and attracts customers who are aware of the ecological aspects of their purchases.

**Practice: TUW PZUW specialists**
**Company: PZU**
**Industry: Finance**
**Year: 2020**

Power plants in cooperation with TUW PZUW (owned by PZU) offered their customers a product called 'TUW PZUW Professionals', which consisted in providing repair services for various home devices and installations in the event of a failure. This service allowed customers to benefit from professional support to repair electrical devices (such as TVs, household appliances and computers), heating and air conditioning equipment, internal electrical, gas, water and sewage installations, and doors, locks and other home items. The benefit of this service was not only lower repair costs but also a more environmentally friendly approach that allowed the life of home appliances to be extended. The effectiveness of this initiative was measured by the amount of gross premiums collected, which came to over PLN

90 million in November 2020. The value of the repairs exceeded PLN 15 million in the same period, which translated into over 38,000 interventions by specialists (PZU, 2021).

The cooperation between energy companies and TUW PZUW promoted sustainable marketing by, among other things, extending the life cycle of products and ecological support. The initiative focused more on the upkeep and maintenance of equipment than on typical sustainable marketing, which focuses on ecological, social and ethical issues in a marketing strategy. However, promoting the lifespan of equipment and energy efficiency had a positive impact on both the environment and customers.

**Practice: Old into new – circular economy**
**Company: Auchan Retail Polska**
**Industry: Trade**
**Year: 2021**

As part of its annual 'Back to School' campaign, Auchan introduced a responsible offer offering FSC (Forest Stewardship Council)-certified environmentally friendly products made of recycled materials and the option to purchase without unnecessary packaging. However, the campaign is not only about the product offer. Auchan also cooperates with Wtórpol and the Eco Textil Foundation. From 5 August to 18 August 2021, customers in Auchan shops had the opportunity to return their old school backpacks or school bags at the Customer Service Point. In return, they received a voucher to purchase a new backpack with a 25% discount. Old backpacks in good condition were reused and those unusable were recycled. During the two weeks of the campaign, 1,014 kg of backpacks were collected in Auchan shops, which translates into over 2,000 pieces. Backpacks in good condition found their way to second-hand clothing stores and will be reused. Those that cannot be reused will be recycled according to the zero-waste principle. The 'Replace your old backpack with a new one' campaign is multidimensional. It is implemented in accordance with the principles of the circular economy, which means repairing, reusing and recycling, and is in line with Auchan's environmental protection policies, reducing its water consumption and carbon footprint. Thanks to this, resources are used rationally and the amount of waste is reduced. The campaign also takes into account the social aspect of environmentalism through support and cooperation with local communities. An important element is education of children and young people, showing them that they can influence the condition of our planet. Funds obtained from the sale and recycling of backpacks are allocated to specialised rehabilitation equipment for those in need (Auchan Retail Polska, 2022).

These practices of Auchan as part of the 'Back to School' campaign demonstrate many features of sustainable marketing such as a responsible product offer, the option of purchasing without unnecessary packaging, partnership with companies with similar values and aims, application of the principles of the circular economy, initiatives for those in need and education of children and young people.

**Practice: Guaranteed repairability of Tefal products for up to 10 years and circular management of equipment in Tefal stores**
**Company: Groupe SEB Polska**
**Industry: Electronics and household appliances**
**Year: 2021**

Tefal aims to ensure that its products can be repaired throughout Europe for up to 10 years and that spare parts are available for 10 years from the date of production. The products are designed to be easily disassembled and reassembled. In Poland, Tefal has established cooperation with Plenti App, enabling the renting of household appliances originating from complaints or the 'Satisfaction Guaranteed' programme. Customers can test the devices at home and if they change their mind return them within 30 days for the purchase price. Returned products, after regeneration, are sold at special prices in the Ursus store, thus avoiding the generation of e-waste. Since 2016, 95% of Tefal products launched are repairable and 24% of them, with the exception of one or two hard-to-find parts, can be repaired at a reasonable cost. Under the 'Satisfaction Guaranteed' programme, Tefal customers return less than 10% of products. The Tefal store in Ursus has sold 50 pieces of regenerated and remanufactured returned' products. The company consistently implements its commitments to the environment and consumers by designing durable products that can be repaired for 10 years from the date of production. This allows consumers to act responsibly and circularly, as the cost of repair is often lower than the cost of purchasing a new product. They can also purchase used but fully functional products that have been returned by other customers at attractive prices. Additionally, when products are no longer suitable to be repaired, consumers can take advantage of the 'Skutecznie posprzątane' (effectively cleaned up) programme by returning electronic waste in Tefal stores and receiving a discount of up to PLN 100 on subsequent purchases (Dobre praktyki CSR w Polsce, 2023).

Tefal's practices demonstrate many of the characteristics of sustainable marketing, indicating that the company engages in activities that balance business aims with concern for the environment and consumer welfare. Sustainable marketing is manifested in long-term durability of products, designing products for repairing and recycling, rental and regeneration of equipment, promotion of repairing, minimisation of returns, social responsibility and education, and discounts on purchases.

**Practice: Responsibly introducing products to the market**
**Company: Groupe SEB Polska**
**Industry: Electronics and household appliances**
**Year: 2021**

The Tefal brand has implemented a sustainable approach to bringing products to market using circular solutions. Household appliances that are not suitable for sale but are fully functional (e.g., returned under a 'Satisfaction Guaranteed' promotion, which allows you to return a product after 30 days of use) are reused in an equipment rental programme in cooperation with the Plenti application (https://plenti.app/pl/products?query=tefal). The idea of sharing equipment instead of owning it is another step towards rationally and sustainably introducing new products to the market. An online platform allows you to rent equipment without having to purchase it. Tefal offers as many as 41 device models in Plenti. This solution is dedicated to people who rarely cook and avoid unnecessary purchases of equipment, which helps to limit the introduction of new devices that could be unused to the market. During the eight months of the Tefal and Plenti project in 2021, 116 people benefited from it. For Groupe SEB, owner of the Tefal brand, which sells over 360 million products worldwide, this commitment to sustainability means great responsibility. The manufacturer promotes sustainable development by making part of its range available on the Plenti platform for people who do not want or cannot purchase equipment. Thanks to these circular policies, Tefal gives a second life to equipment that was returned to the company by consumers as a result of a complaint or as part of the 'Satisfaction Guaranteed' programme (Dobre praktyki CSR w Polsce, 2023).

These practices of the Tefal brand clearly manifest a sustainable approach to marketing and business activities in the form of a developed circular model, renting instead of buying equipment, cooperation with the Plenti application, limiting the generation of e-waste, social responsibility, maintaining a balance between profit and sustainable development.

**Practice: Collecting used shoes 'Give your shoes a second life'**
**Company: CCC Group**
**Industry: Trade**
**Year: 2021**

CCC has continued its 'Give your shoes a second life' campaign, which was launched in 2020 and involves collecting used footwear from customers and employees. CCC shops in Poland have special containers where you can deposit unused shoes. The donated footwear is analysed for the possibility of recovery and reuse. The company rewards customers with discount vouchers for each complete pair of shoes donated for collection. In addition, CCC has organised a shoe collection among employees in partnership with WoshWosh, donating shoes to homeless people. Currently, there are collection containers available in many CCC shops in Poland, and the company plans to expand the programme to all its shops in Poland and abroad. In 2021, over 6,000 pairs of shoes were collected, of which 3,000 were donated to homeless people thanks to the WoshWosh campaign, and over 3,000 were placed in containers in CCC shops. Since the beginning of the campaign in 2020, CCC has collected nearly

13,000 pairs of used shoes. These practices support sustainable development goals, including management of used footwear and introducing the concept of closed product circulation. Thanks to the shoe collection, customers can donate unused shoes in an environmentally friendly way, and CCC ensures their proper management (CCC, 2022).

Sustainable marketing in CCC's activities is manifested in collecting and reusing products, rewarding customers, cooperating with a charity and expanding the programme.

**Practice: Circular economy**
**Company: Hochland**
**Industry: Food**
**Year: 2021**

In 2021, Hochland introduced a number of practices aimed at giving objects a second life. On the occasion of 'No Litter Day' Hochland carried out an e-waste collection campaign, in which employees donated e-waste. After appropriate processing, the raw material collected was reused to create new products. A total of 670 kg of e-waste was collected. At the beginning of September, the company organised a campaign to issue used high-quality office furniture to avoid waste. This was combined with a collection of funds for those in need. In mid-September, Hochland cooperated with STENA Recycling to collect shoes for homeless people. Fifty-five pairs of shoes were collected and donated to people in need. Additionally, the company joined the world clean-up campaign with the slogan 'I will show culture, eat cheese and protect nature', during which 300 kg of waste was collected. These actions helped reduce waste and improve the natural environment while increasing the standard of living of those in need (Hochland, 2022).

In the practices of the Hochland company, sustainable marketing is manifested in the following ways: collection of electronic waste and footwear for those in need, distribution of used furniture and a clean-up-the-world campaign. These practices demonstrate that Hochland is committed to sustainable practices while caring for the natural environment and the community. It promotes the recovery of raw materials, minimising waste and supporting people in need, which is an important element in sustainable marketing.

**Practice: Exchanging used smartphones**
**Company: T-Mobile Polska**
**Industry: Telecommunications**
**Year: 2021**

Reconciling the interests of consumers and environmental protection is a challenge. Therefore, in 2021 T-Mobile started to sell used smartphones in a programme called 'Smartphone Regeneration'. As part of this campaign, customers who brought used devices to showrooms received attractive repurchase offers. Moreover, the company assured customers that old devices would be refurbished and sent to new users or used as parts for production.

T-Mobile assesses the effectiveness of this practice based on the number of phones purchased (trade-in campaign) and the number of second-hand phones sold (Smartphone ReGeneracja). The main benefit of this initiative is that it extends the life of electronic products and customer education on pro-ecological activities (T-Mobile Polska, 2022).

The main elements of sustainable marketing by T-Mobile are promoting recycling, renewing and reusing products, monitoring the effectiveness of activities and educating customers about pro-ecological activities (T-Mobile Polska, 2021).

**Practice: Circular Economy**
**Company: Walstead Central Europe/Walstead Kraków**
**Industry: Wood, paper and furniture**
**Year: 2021**

The company introduced CHEP (Commonwealth Handling Equipment Pool) pallets to the market with reusable pallets, replacing cardboard packaging and wrapping with reusable boxes. In an offset printing process, the company uses water in a closed circuit, filtering and reusing used water. In addition, the company is testing nets made of durable Green Spider material to protect pallets during transport and storage. Thanks to these activities, the company has reduced orders for pallets and boxes, saving water and reducing plastic waste and stretch film consumption. The introduction of CHEP pallets also helps reduce $CO_2$ emissions and protect the natural environment through closed water circulation and minimising the amount of industrial waste (Dobre praktyki CSR w Polsce, 2023).

Walstead Central Europe/Walstead Kraków has implemented such elements of sustainable marketing as reducing raw material consumption, efficient use of resources, reduction of $CO_2$ emissions and protection of the natural environment. By taking these actions, the company contributes to sustainable development and meets the expectations of customers interested in environmentally friendly products and services.

**Practice: Circular economy**
**Company: City of Krakow waterworks (MPO)**
**Industry: Water and sewage**
**Year: 2021**

The circular economy is important for environmental protection. An example of an effective circular economy is reuse of treated sewage after additional filtration and disinfection to produce process water. In this way, it is possible to avoid using drinking water for technological purposes and to use this water for washing streets in Krakow. Cooperation between the City of Krakow waterworks and the MPO Sp. z o. o. promotes sustainable development. The efficiency indicators are the amount of process water purchased by MPO Sp. z o. o. and the amount of water used for internal technological purposes. The benefit is saving water resources because the reuse of water for technological purposes has significantly reduced the consumption of drinking water in sewage treatment plants in Płaszów and Kujawy (Dobre praktyki CSR w Polsce, 2023).

City of Krakow waterworks includes various elements of sustainable marketing in its practices, such as a circular economy, reuse of resources, avoiding wasting drinking water, cooperation between companies, use of performance indicators and benefits from activities.

**Practice: IKEA promotes refreshing and repairing sofas**
**Company: IKEA Retail**
**Industry: Wood, paper and furniture**
**Year: 2021**

IKEA is actively seeking to transform its traditional business model into a more sustainable circular model. It is achieving this through a range of activities, including designing products and services to minimise the environmental impact. One of the key elements in this approach is enabling customers to make sustainable consumer decisions. An example is offering spare parts for sofas. Customers who purchased a sofa from IKEA can now refresh and repair their furniture instead of replacing it with a new one. The shop offers not only spare parts for sofas but also various types of covers, legs and accessories that allow you to change the appearance of the furniture. This sensible approach helps extend the life cycle of furniture, which in turn leads to a significant reduction in waste. IKEA evaluates the effectiveness of this programme using the level of sales of spare parts for sofas. After the test phase of the project, these parts became a permanent element in the company's sales offer. The benefit of this solution is not only a sustainable approach to purchasing but also a reduction in potential waste that would be generated when getting rid of old furniture and purchasing new furniture. IKEA encourages customers to repair and renovate furniture themselves, which promotes the circular economy and fits the zero-waste idea (Dobre praktyki CSR w Polsce, 2023).

IKEA demonstrates a sustainable approach in its operations by designing products with the environment in mind, enabling customers to make sustainable choices, extending product life cycles, assessing the effectiveness of operations and promoting zero-waste practices. This is an example of a company that actively pursues sustainable development and engages customers in the process of achieving this goal.

**Practice: Green Black Friday**
**Company: IKEA Retail**
**Industry: Wood, paper and furniture**
**Year: 2021**

IKEA Retail in Poland has long been promoting conscious shopping on Black Friday. In the past, it has proposed unusual collections such as 'PRZYDA SIĘ' with things we already have, and a 'For longer' campaign, encouraging people to take care of the items they own. In this year's 'Give back and gain' campaign, IKEA allowed customers to return old IKEA furniture, which goes to a circular hub to find a new life through resale. This is an initiative that points the way to more sustainable consumption and less use of the planet's resources. During the campaign, IKEA examined results that were considered promising, such as the number of customers using it, the amount of returned furniture, the average value of refund cards and the percentage of furniture that found a 'second life'. This campaign is one of IKEA's sustainability efforts and is an important step in reducing the use of natural resources by extending the life of existing furniture. It is also a response to customer expectations regarding business support in taking more environmentally friendly actions. The Green Black Friday campaign confirms that taking care of the planet does not have to be expensive (Dobre praktyki CSR w Polsce, 2023).

IKEA in Poland uses sustainable marketing by promoting conscious purchases, unusual collections, campaigns encouraging people to take care of their items, initiatives supporting the circular economy, analysing the effectiveness of activities and providing customers with wallet-friendly solutions. These policies support sustainable development and contribute to reducing negative impacts on the environment.

**Practice: CSR strategy for companies**
**Company: KNK Productions & Development**
**Industry: Clothing**
**Year: 2021**

By implementing the UPDIWU (Upcycle Do It With Us) CSR tool, conscientious brands have an opportunity to offer customers innovative solutions in the field of upcycling clothing. This is not only about selling finished products but also about building an aware community involved in upcycling in the fashion industry. Customers who purchase these ready-made products have the opportunity to modify them, for example, by dyeing or refreshing them, using UPDIWU CSR tools. In this way, clothing brands show understanding and concern for sustainable production, and their customers can be sure that they are buying valuable products made in a sustainable way. The effectiveness of this approach is monitored with specific UPDIWU CSR tool targets and monthly reports focusing on the number of companies receiving support, finished products processed, lectures and events promoting UPDIWU CSR. Additionally, long-term effects include increasing the number of UPDIWU CSR participants and spreading CSR awareness in upcycling clothing in the textile industry. Monitoring the results of practices using UPDIWU CSR tools aims to assess the effectiveness of the targets set and helps determine interest in the products on the domestic and international markets. For customers who introduce the UPDIWU CSR tool in their business, it brings a number of benefits, such as innovations in the market, strengthening competitiveness and recognition, greater customer loyalty, strengthening relationships with customers, gaining new customers, gaining public trust, reducing environmental impacts, increasing awareness of the brand as socially responsible and the use of the best upcycling techniques available in the Polish market (Dobre praktyki CSR w Polsce, 2023).

The practices described demonstrate that KNK Productions & Development implements sustainable marketing by promoting clothing upcycling, engaging customers, offering upcycling tools and monitoring the effectiveness of policies and long-term aims. This approach contributes to sustainable consumption, customer education and the promotion of responsible fashion.

**Practice: Supporting the circular economy**
**Company: Nhood Polska**
**Industry: Construction and real estate**
**Year: 2021**

Nhood Polska actively promotes the principles of the circular economy (reduce, reuse, repair, recycle) among its customers, convincing them of the impact of everyday choices on the climate. In the facilities it manages, it organises various activities and events promoting these principles. Examples of activities include collecting old bicycles and bicycle parts for the 'Mierz Wysoko' association at the Auchan Piaseczno Shopping Centre and Galerią Łomianki near Warsaw. Moreover, its 'Plant Adoption Point' initiative in Krakow's Galeria Bronowice and Galeria Łomianki allows plants to be given names, be watered and find new owners, which contributes to the reuse of these plants. Auchan shopping centres in Gdańsk, Bydgoszcz and Rumia organise creative family workshops in which participants learn how to transform old objects into unique decorations. Moreover, electronic waste collections have been organised at the Auchan Shopping Centre. Thanks to these initiatives, customers of shopping centres managed by Nhood have an opportunity to give a 'second life' to unused objects and plants, which contributes to promotion of the principles of the circular economy (Nhood Polska, 2022).

Nhood Polska promotes the principles of the circular economy, reuse and care for the environment in its managed commercial facilities. These initiatives are examples of sustainable marketing that engages customers and contributes to education and behavioural change towards more sustainable and conscious consumerism.

**Practice: We don't throw away – we pass it on. Pelion Company Market**
**Company: Pelion Group**
**Industry: Pharmaceuticals**
**Year: 2021**

In order to effectively manage resources, Pelion has created a website that allows employees of Group companies to reuse items and office supplies. This initiative was a response to suggestions from employees themselves who had items that they no longer used in their daily work but which could be useful to others, while contributing to reducing procurement costs. The website allows employees to publish various types of offers, such as office supplies and work equipment. The project has a long-term nature and is aimed at promoting the reuse of objects, which contributes to reducing the burden on the natural environment. Pelion encourages employees to join this initiative and contribute to caring for the environment and give objects a second life. The effectiveness of the project is measured by the number of items listed on the online platform. The project started in December 2020 and continued throughout 2021. There are nearly 10 product categories on the website, and the company plans to increase this number over time. This initiative is an expression of Pelion's commitment and responsibility towards the environment. The company takes many actions to minimise negative impacts on the environment in its operations. Pelion manages raw materials effectively, limits the consumption of water, paper, electricity and fuel, as well as applies a waste management policy that respects the environment. Additionally, it promotes pro-ecological attitudes among employees and stakeholders and introduces environmentally friendly behaviour and technological solutions that reduce negative impacts on the environment. For the company's employees, participation in this initiative is an opportunity to actively engage in environmental protection and support sustainable practices, which contributes to caring for the environment and giving objects a second life (Dobre praktyki CSR w Polsce, 2023).

Pelion demonstrates sustainable marketing by creating a platform for reusing items, listening to employee suggestions, promoting reuse, encouraging active participation, measuring the effectiveness of activities and sustainable practices within the company and promoting pro-ecological attitudes. These initiatives support sustainable development goals, educate employees and contribute to a more sustainable and conscientious approach to resource and environmental management.

**Practice: Replacing plastic packaging with more sustainable alternatives**
**Company: Sodexo**
**Industry: Services**
**Year: 2021**

Sodexo has introduced a key element in its strategy, which is eliminating single-use plastic. It has replaced plastic items with eco-friendly alternatives such as wood, paper, cardboard and straw fibres, including cutlery, plates, stirrers and straws. Sodexo has become the largest player in the catering industry in Europe to make such a commitment. The company was ahead of current European Union (EU) regulations on single-use plastic, which came into force on 1 July this year. In Poland, Sodexo has already withdrawn single-use plastic items from over 40 restaurants. In the first stage, five product categories were abandoned: plastic cutlery, plates, stirrers, straws and bags. The next stage is a plan to replace styrofoam and PLA (polylactide) packaging with 100% paper or cane pulp products. Serving over 100 million consumers around the world, Sodexo recognises the role it plays in global efforts to reduce the use of plastics in everyday life. In its offer and activities, it is guided by the principles of a sustainable economy, ensuring that all waste can be reused and preventing waste of raw materials. The company works with local authorities, suppliers and partners to identify opportunities for reuse and increase recycling rates at its facilities. For other plastic items used in food service, such as kitchen containers, takeaway packaging, cups and lids, the company continues to look for sustainable alternatives. Reducing the use of single-use plastic is an additional value that Sodexo wants to provide to its business partners (Sodexo Polska, 2022).

Sodexo's efforts to eliminate single-use plastics and its approach to environmental management and sustainability exemplify sustainable marketing. The company not only takes concrete steps towards environmental protection but also communicates these policies and values to its customers and business partners, which can contribute to building a positive brand image.

**Practice: Innovations in polybags**
**Company: LPP**
**Industry: Clothing**
**Year: 2022**

LPP is increasingly closing the wrapping circuit. When transported by sea to warehouses, clothing travels thousands of kilometres. To protect them from moisture and damage, items are packed in separate plastic bags, which are called polybags in the industry. Since 2021, all LPP polybags have been made from at least 70% recycled polyethylene and are fully recyclable. From 2023, all new orders will be delivered to customers in bags made of 100% recycled polyethylene (rLDPE). Polybags from LPP warehouses and headquarters – along with other collected wrapping – go to the recycler, and they are used to produce waste bags (LPP, 2023).

LPP's practices in the field of sustainable development are consistent with the idea of sustainable marketing. The company implements solutions that contribute to environmental protection, communicates its initiatives and cooperates with other entities. Thanks to this, LPP contributes to promoting sustainable development.

**Practice: Returnable bottles**
**Company: Grupa Żywiec**
**Industry: Food**
**Year: 2022**

By purchasing beer in a returnable bottle, you can contribute to environmental protection. A returnable bottle can be used repeatedly, up to 20 times. This reduces greenhouse gas emissions, which are four times lower than those of an aluminium can and five times more than those of a disposable bottle.

A returnable bottle can be reused without additional processing. After it is returned, it is thoroughly washed and checked for quality. It is then refilled and sent to the store. However, customers who prefer beer in a non-returnable bottle or can are also able to contribute to environmental protection. These containers can be recycled and used to produce new ones. Recycling allows you to save natural raw materials. New glass bottles consist of an average of 40–80% cullet material, and aluminium cans contain an average of 70% recycled aluminium. Aluminium cans and glass bottles do not lose their properties during recycling. They just need to be dropped in the appropriate containers. Therefore, Grupa Żywiec encourages you to buy beer in a returnable bottle or to recycle beer containers. These are simple actions that have a real impact on environmental protection (Grupa Żywiec, 2022).

To sum up, Grupa Żywiec undertakes such activities as promoting reusable packaging, encouraging recycling and informing about the impact of its activities on the environment. These initiatives are consistent with the idea of sustainable marketing, which aims to integrate marketing with environmental protection.

**Practice: Recycled household products**
**Company: Lidl Poland**
**Industry: Trade**
**Year: 2022**

Lidl Polska and PreZero, a company belonging to the Schwarz Group, cooperate to produce household products from 100% recycled plastic. PreZero collects packaging waste from households, sorts it by type of material, cleans it and processes it into granules. This secondary raw material is then used to produce household goods packaging, plastic bags, rubbish bags and stretch films. The entire recycling and production process takes place in Europe, which reduces $CO_2$ emissions (Lidl Polska, 2022).

Lidl's sustainable marketing is manifested in reducing the consumption of natural resources and the amount of waste and promoting environmental protection and sustainable development.

**Practice: Sustainable packaging and delivery**
**Company: Allegro**
**Industry: E-commerce**
**Year: 2022**

Allegro actively strives to achieve sustainable development by implementing initiatives related to renewable energy, sustainable supply and education on climate issues. The company has shown that e-commerce generates significantly lower emissions compared to traditional shops, underlining its commitment to the fight against climate change. Allegro has ambitious climate aims in line with scientific standards and has raised its MSCI (Morgan Stanley Capital International Indices) environmental, social and governance (ESG) rating. In addition, the company has introduced innovative solutions related to sustainable packaging and delivery and cooperates with various ecological initiatives to protect the environment. Allegro also puts great emphasis on educating customers and employees in the field of sustainable development (Allegro.pl, 2023).

Allegro is actively involved in environmental protection and combating climate change, which delivers significant results including reducing greenhouse gas emissions across the value chain by 10.4%; obtaining 23% of energy from renewable sources thanks to guarantees of origin; annually reducing greenhouse gas emissions by 12.2%; reducing emission intensity across the value chain relative to revenue by an impressive 28%; introducing 3.7 million items of ecological packaging to the market; and effectively recycling 98% of waste from Allegro warehouses. These achievements underline Allegro's commitment to creating sustainable solutions and shaping a greener future.

**Practice: ESG products and services**
**Company: mBank SA**
**Industry: Finance**
**Year: 2022**

ESG products and services focus on promoting and providing clients with financial solutions that take into account aspects of sustainable development, including eco-mortgage loans; loans for ecological purposes for entrepreneurs; recycled payment cards; planet-friendly leasing; renewable energy financing; ESG-compliant investing; and green bonds (mBank S.A, 2023).

Additionally, mBank is involved in sustainable marketing through customer education, cooperation with social organisations, publishing reports on sustainable business, employing ethical marketing practices and minimising negative impacts on the environment. These activities help the bank build a positive image, attract customers and support the aims of sustainable social and ecological development.

**Practice: Climate change and the natural environment**
**Company: Budimex Group**
**Industry: Construction**
**Year: 2022**

For the Budimex Group, practice in the field of climate change and environmental protection is an important element of sustainable development and corporate social responsibility (CSR). The Budimex Group, one of the largest construction companies in Poland, is aware of the impact of its activities on the natural environment and the need to counteract climate change. The most important aspects of its practice in this area are sustainable construction; waste management; nature conservation; emissions reduction; employee education and involvement; and monitoring and reporting (Budimex SA, 2023).

The activities of the Budimex Group in the field of climate change and environmental protection in the context of sustainable marketing can be characterised as marketing sustainable construction projects; ecological communication; partnerships with environmental organisations; shaping consumer attitudes; reporting on progress; and using sustainable construction certificates. These practices allow the Budimex Group to build a positive image as a company that cares about the natural environment and is committed to solving climate-related problems, which may attract customers, investors and business partners who share these values.

## 4.3 Conclusions

To summarise the examples analysed, it should be noted that the circular economy, which focuses on minimizing waste and maximising the use of resources through recycling, reusing and reducing consumption, is definitely gaining popularity. Circular practices are becoming more and more common, and brands are increasingly boasting about the economic, social and environmental results they achieve. Companies have begun to realize that caring for the natural environment not only affects their image but can also contribute to cost savings and long-term sustainability. In the area of marketing practices, more and more companies in Poland in more and more industries have started to emphasize their sustainable activities in marketing communications. Customers have begun to attach more importance to purchasing from companies that care about the environment, which in turn encourages companies to adapt their marketing strategies to these expectations. Future projections indicate a continued increase in interest in the circular economy, especially in the context of growing public awareness of environmental issues. Businesses that invest in sustainable practices can expect benefits in terms of both reputation and operational efficiency. During this work, special attention has been paid to how to use methodically designed green marketing activities to influence pro-ecological behaviour and attitudes and motivate sustainable consumption. Such activities may create additional values for customers, such as a sense of fulfilling a socially expected obligation to care for the environment. Promoting ecological awareness and encouraging ecologically responsible activities can and should always be supported by solutions and marketing activities. This will enable the creation of the most valuable content possible, facilitating the implementation of beneficial solutions, characterised primarily by readability and visibility of signing and encouraging immersive involvement in projects by everyone. It will also influence the need for large corporations to take such actions into account because they will be expected and even required by customers and society at large. The green marketing solutions, tools and recommendations developed will also contribute to activities in the field of sustainable development, in particular, to more effectively educate society about the need to take into account the principles of sustainable development during everyday consumer decisions and habits; more accurate and visible signalling of activities carried out in the field of sustainable development, and also of awards and distinctions received, which will have a positive impact on creating the image of socially responsible brands; promoting the principles of proper waste segregation and recycling, with among other things, properly designed visible easy-to-interpret labelling; and promoting green behaviour, including the use of reusable packaging and biodegradable ecologically 'clean' materials.

Nowadays, enterprises are increasingly paying attention to the idea of a circular economy, which is a response to the growing challenges related to environmental protection and natural resources. This chapter has discussed practical examples of enterprise activities in the circular economy which have implemented sustainable marketing solutions and practices. Additionally, available European government and social programmes supporting pro-ecological market development have been reviewed. As a summary, it is worth pointing out the key conditions for, advantages and disadvantages of practices, together with recommendations for practitioners interested in implementing sustainable marketing in their enterprises.

In terms of conditions, it is worth paying special attention to increasing ecological awareness. Customers are becoming more and more aware of the impact of their behaviour on the environment. This forces companies to redefine their practices and offerings. Additional regulations and provisions that introduce increasingly strict regulations regarding the circular economy mean that enterprises must adapt to new standards. Moreover, within the concept of sustainable development, companies recognise both the ecological and economic benefits of more sustainable practices, which encourages practices working towards a circular economy.

Disadvantages include investment costs: transitioning to circular economy models often requires investing in new infrastructure and technologies, which may initially generate high costs. In addition, there are difficulties in managing sources of secondary raw materials. This and recycling can be challenging, especially for larger companies. The final barrier is possible resistance by consumers, because despite a high level of awareness, some consumers may not be ready for changes in products or services related to the circular economy, which may constitute an obstacle.

The undoubted advantages are saving raw materials and energy, creating a positive image, innovation and competitiveness. A circular economy allows for more efficient use of raw materials and energy, which translates into lower costs and fewer burdens on the environment. Companies engaging in the circular economy can build a positive image as ecologically responsible companies, which attracts customers and investors. Striving for sustainable operations can stimulate innovation and increase the competitiveness of companies in the market.

Therefore, companies should carefully analyse the life cycle of their products and services to identify areas where sustainable practices can be introduced. Collaboration with suppliers, customers and other companies can contribute to the successful implementation of sustainable solutions. It is worth investing in consumer education to increase their awareness and acceptance of sustainable practices and encourage them to make more ecological choices. Additionally, regularly monitoring performance and publishing reports on circular economy policies can help build customer and investor confidence.

As part of this work, in-depth case study-based research was conducted to explore sustainable marketing practices in various companies. The information contained in the cases was based on activities declared by the companies, and these data were obtained by conducting interviews with company representatives and analysing documents, such as, among other things, CSR reports. In many cases, the sustainable marketing practices presented by the companies surveyed concerned specific activities undertaken as part of the circular economy. Some companies focused on individual initiatives in the field of recycling, emission reduction or the introduction of ecological products. An important factor was that not all the companies surveyed presented coherent sustainable development strategies but focused on individual activities. One of the key findings concerned the motivations for companies to adopt this approach. In some cases, there is a tendency to take individual actions related to sustainable marketing, which may indicate some greenwashing practices. The question therefore arises of whether these companies are just trying to adapt their activities to customer expectations of sustainable companies or whether these individual steps are the initial stages in a long-term strategy. When companies communicate their sustainable marketing practices, do they really want to contribute to positive change or are they just trying to please increasingly environmentally conscious consumers? Analysing these issues can shed light on companies' true intentions and help understand whether these are genuine sustainability efforts or merely efforts to improve the company's image.

To sum up, the circular economy is becoming an increasingly important aspect of business operations. Despite some challenges, the benefits for both the environment and the businesses themselves are significant. Market practitioners should invest in innovative solutions and education to achieve success in sustainable marketing and initiatives based on the idea of a circular economy and in order to achieve full effectiveness and credibility of activities, ensure their long-term implementation within a framework of developed strategies and not only individual activities.

## References

Allegro.pl (2023). *Raport ESG 2022 #SustainableAllTogether*. https://raportyzr.pl/wp-content/uploads/2023/09/SustainableAllTogether_Allegro2022_PL.pdf (accessed 24.10.2023).

Anwil (2020). *Raport Odpowiedzialny Biznes w Polsce. Dobre praktyki 2019*. https://odpowiedzialnybiznes.pl/wp-content/uploads/2020/04/FOB_Raport2019.pdf (accessed 26.09.2023).

Auchan Retail Polska (2022). *Razem odpowiedzialni. Raport CSR 2020–2021*. https://aristorsmi001.blob.core.windows.net/cms-content/pl/2020/04/Auchan_raport-CSR_2020-2021-1-1.pdf (accessed 23.09.2023).

BASF (2020). *BASF sfinalizował inwestycję w Środzie Śląskiej*. https://www.basf.com/pl/pl/media/news-releases/2019/06/basf-sfinalizowa-inwestycj-w-rodzie-lskiej.html (accessed 26.09.2023).

Budimex, SA (2023). *Raport zintegrowany Grupy Budimex za rok 2022, Dla ludzi. Dla lepszego życia*. https://raportyzr.pl/wp-content/uploads/2023/09/raport-zintegrowany-2022.pdf (accessed 25.10.2023).

Carlsberg (2020). *Zero water waste*. https://www.carlsberggroup.com/sustainability/our-esg-programme/zero-water-waste/ (accessed 26.09.2023).

Carrefour Polska (2019). *Commiting to eco-design and a circular economy for packaging*. https://www.carrefour.com/sites/default/files/2020-08/Committing%20to%20ecodesign.pdf (accessed 26.09.2023).

CCC (2022). *Daj swoim butom drugie życie*. https://ccc.eu/pl/daj-swoim-butom-drugie-zycie (accessed 26.09.2023).

CCC Group (2021). *EXPERIENCCCE. Raport zrównoważonego rozwoju Grupy Kapitałowej CCC za rok obrotowy rozpoczynający się 1 lutego 2021 r., zakończony 31 stycznia 2022 r*. https://corporate.ccc.eu/raporty-esg (accessed 22.09.2023).

Creswell, J. W. (2007). *Qualitative Inquiry and Research Design: Choosing among Five Approaches*. Thousand Oaks: Sage Publications.

Ćwiklicki, M., & Urbaniak, A. (2019). *Studium przypadku w naukach o zarządzaniu*. Kraków: Wydawnictwo Uniwersytetu Ekonomicznego w Krakowie.

Dobre praktyki CSR w Polsce (2023). https://odpowiedzialnybiznes.pl/dobre-praktyki/ (accessed 20–23.09.2023).

Eneris (2020). *Rowerowy upcykling w Gorzowie*. https://eneris.pl/informacje-dla-prasy/aktualnosci/rowerowy-upcykling-gorzowie (accessed 26.09.2023).

ERGO Hestia (2021). *Troska. Raport zrównoważonego rozwoju. Grupa ERGO Hestia 2020*. https://cdn.bsbox.pl/files/hestia/YjM7MDA_/356d57202191a4c273a2bd50eeb43b16_documents-bb48af6e-6cc8-4a80-8787-bc41e5b417e1.pdf (accessed 25.09.2023).

Forum Odpowiedzialnego Biznesu (2020). *Raport Odpowiedzialny Biznes w Polsce. Dobre praktyki 2020*. https://odpowiedzialnybiznes.pl/wp-content/uploads/2021/04/FOB_Raport2020.pdf (accessed 26.09.2023).

Forum Odpowiedzialnego Biznesu (2021). *Raport Odpowiedzialny biznes w Polsce 2021. Dobre praktyki*. https://odpowiedzialnybiznes.pl/publikacje/raport-2021/ (accessed 26.09.2023).

Grupa Żywiec (2022). *Sprawozdanie na temat informacji niefinansowych Grupy Żywiec S.A. oraz Grupy Kapitałowej Żywiec S.A. za rok 2022*. https://raportyzr.pl/wp-content/uploads/2023/09/2022.pdf (accessed 25.09.2023).

Henkel Polska (2019). *Henkel announces ambitious targets for sustainable packaging*. https://www.henkel.pl/prasa-media/informacje-materialy-prasowe/2018-09-03-henkel-announces-ambitious-targets-for-sustainable-packaging-873418 (accessed 26.09.2023).

Hochland (2022). *Raport zrównoważonego rozwoju Hochland Polska* 2021. https://www.hochland-group.com/pl/downloads/Raport%20Hochland%20PL.pdf (accessed 21.09.2023).

IKEA (2020). *Razem urządzamy lepszy świat.* https://habitat.pl/ikea/o-projekcie/ (accessed 26.09.2023).

ING Bank Śląski (2019). *Billboard na plecach? Nerka z recyclingu? W ING dajemy reklamom drugie życie.* https://spolecznosc.ing.pl/-/Blog/Billboard-na-plecach-Nerka-z-recyclingu-W-ING-dajemy-reklamom/ba-p/20382 (accessed 26.09.2023).

ING Bank Śląski (2020). *Zintegrowany Raport Roczny ING Banku Śląskiego 2020.* https://raportyzr.pl/wp-content/uploads/2021/08/IngRaport22PL2.pdf (accessed 25.09.2023).

ING Bank Śląski (2021). *Rethinking the road to the circular economy.* https://think.ing.com/reports/circular-economy-rounding-up-the-costs-and-benefits (accessed 26.09.2023).

Intive (2020). *Add Zero Waste to your office relocation checklist.* https://intive.com/insights/add-zero-waste-to-your-office-relocation-checklist (accessed 26.09.2023).

Jula (2020). *Another Men's Shed in collaboration with Jula.* https://retailmarketexperts.com/en/news/another-mens-shed-in-collaboration-with-jula/ (accessed 26.09.2023).

Kaufland Polska Markety (2020). *Skrzynki wielorazowego użytku dla gospodarki w obiegu zamkniętym.* https://odpowiedzialnybiznes.pl/dobre-praktyki/skrzynki-wielorazowego-uzytku-dla-gospodarki-w-obiegu-zamknietym/ (accessed 26.09.2023).

L'Oréal Polska (2019). *Articles: Sharing Beauty with All.* https://www.loreal.com/en/articles/l-oreal-pour-le-futur/?page=5 (accessed 26.09.2023).

Lafarge (2019). *Lafarge Poland opens ash separation plant in Siekierki.* https://www.globalcement.com/news/item/7889-lafarge-poland-opens-ash-separation-plant-in-siekierki (accessed 26.09.2023).

Lidl Polska (2022). *Raport zrównoważonego rozwoju Lidl Polska. Lata obrotowe 2021–2022.* https://raportyzr.pl/wp-content/uploads/2023/09/Raport-Zrownowazonego-Rozwoju-Lidl-Polska-2021-2022_small.pdf (accessed 25.09.2023).

LPP (2023). *Sprawozdanie zrównoważonego rozwoju za rok 2022/2023. W kierunku gospodarki cyrkularnej.* https://raportyzr.pl/wp-content/uploads/2023/09/LPP-Sprawozdanie-zrownowazonego-rozwoju-za-rok-2022-2023-PL.pdf (accessed 26.09.2023).

mBank S.A (2023). Raport ESG 2022 mBank S.A. https://raportyzr.pl/wp-content/uploads/2023/09/mbank-raport-esg-za-2022.pdf (accessed 24.10.2023).

MindBlowing (2020). *Raport Odpowiedzialny Biznes w Polsce. Dobre praktyki 2019.* https://odpowiedzialnybiznes.pl/wp-content/uploads/2020/04/FOB_Raport2019.pdf (accessed 26.09.2023).

Nhood Polska (2022). *Raport zrównoważonego rozwoju Nhood Polska za 2021 rok.* https://nhood.pl/wp-content/uploads/2022/05/CSR_Nhood_za_2021.pdf (accessed 26.09.2023).

PZU (2021). Pomoc fachowca. https://klubpzupomoc.pzu.pl/uslugi-pzu-pomoc/pomoc-fachowca (accessed 26.09.2023).

Sodexo Polska (2022). *Raport Społecznej Odpowiedzialności Biznesu 2021.* https://issuu.com/sodexopl/docs/sodexo_polska_-_raport_spo_ecznej_o_e0a14da3cb7546 (accessed 24.09.2023).

T-Mobile Polska (2021). *Raport zrównoważonego rozwoju 2020.* https://raport-t-mobile-polska.pl/ (accessed 20.09.2023).

T-Mobile Polska (2022). *Raport zrównoważonego rozwoju 2021.* https://raport-t-mobile-polska.pl/wp-content/uploads/2022/09/TmobileRaport21.pdf (accessed 20.09.2023).

Urtica (2021). Dajemy drugie życie komputerom. https://www.urticadzieciom.pl/dajemy-drugie-zycie-komputerom/ (accessed 20.09.2023).

Veolia (2020). *Local loops of energy*. https://www.veolia.com/sites/g/files/dvc4206/files/document/2021/11/local-loops-energy-veolia-en.pdf (accessed 26.09.2023).

Veolia Group (2020). *Produkcja i dystrybucja ciepła w Miasteczku Śląskim*. https://www.veolia.pl/nasza-oferta/referencje/produkcja-i-dystrybucja-ciepla-w-miasteczku-slaskim (accessed 26,09.2023).

Wosh Wosh (2020). *Masz zbędne zimowe buty w szafie? Dzięki polskiej firmie trafią do potrzebujących*. https://innpoland.pl/163433,zbiorka-butow-zimowych-bezdomni-czekaja-na-pomoc (accessed 26.09.2023).

Yin, R. K. R. K. (2015). *Studium przypadku w badaniach naukowych. Projektowanie i metody*. Kraków: Wydawnictwo Uniwersytetu Jagiellońskiego.

Żabka (2021). *Wygodnie i odpowiedzialnie. Raport Odpowiedzialności Żabka Polska Sp. z o. o. za rok 202a0*. https://raportyzr.pl/wp-content/uploads/2021/08/Raport_Odpowiedzialnosci_Zabka_Polska_Sp_z_o_o_-za-_rok-2020.pdf (accessed 26.09.2023).

# Conclusions

Going skiing in the winter is an important part of life for much of Polish society. Every year, a topic of conversation in December in Poland is whether Christmas will be white. It is increasingly noticeable that snow is no longer a frequent part of the winter landscape. There are, of course, more pronounced climate changes that we notice during our lifetime. Some of them we welcome and some we object to or fear. Over the years it has become common knowledge that the global climate situation requires changes in human behaviour because overexploitation of the environment is beginning to result in a significant reduction in human well-being. However, the accustomed patterns of behaviour of individual community members and the lack of more substantial pressure to change them and of institutional support for change make it difficult to stop the spiral of environmental deterioration. This uncontrolled satisfaction of needs is associated with a misallocation of resources and the heavy burden of these decisions on the rest of humanity. Observing global changes allows one to understand deep social injustices and imbalances.

Sustainable marketing is an attractive idea for businesses and consumers who care about sustainability. It involves a package of evident ideals and assumptions, the wording of which is complicated to argue with. At a declarative level, the public's attitude to the idea of sustainable marketing looks very good. However, the complexity of the measures required to enable comprehensive implementation of these ideals in practice makes it a challenge beyond the capabilities of some groups of individual consumers and businesses, mainly because implementation of the concept can have various results.

The decision-making process in sustainable marketing requires comprehensive analysis and inclusion of more information than traditional marketing approaches. The analysis should include the results of decisions which are very much deferred in time and subject to a high risk of error. The risk stems primarily from an inability to estimate fashion trends determining interest in a company's offerings. Other important risk factors include a lack of predictability regarding technical innovations that can help make more sustainable decisions. New inventions are appearing increasingly rapidly and can result in some production technologies being sometimes quite unexpectedly declared

DOI: 10.4324/9781003408642-6

obsolete and harmful to the environment. An example is the history of using energy sources in the 20th and 21st centuries.

Interest in fossil fuels, nuclear energy and renewable energy sources is sometimes almost sinusoidal. The popularity of these solutions very much depends on the context, for example, on assessments of the safety of using them (nuclear energy), the social dimension (closing coal mines and laying off workers) and potential harm to some aspects of the environment (clean wind energy is also noisy, which causes discomfort to nearby humans and animals). In addition, one should add energy security and the management of waste that occurs with these technologies (raw material waste and used machinery and equipment). For example, nuclear energy is considered zero-emission at the time it is generated but it is a source of radioactive waste, and zero-emission electric cars are a source of used batteries, which require complicated and expensive disposal after use. The context of evaluations of selected solutions strongly influences their outcomes.

The development of sustainable marketing depends on the ability to collect and analyse data to help make marketing decisions. Big data provide opportunities for extensive ex-post analysis but limited forecasting of how certain decisions affect the surrounding reality. The limitation of this forecasting is primarily due to changes in the environment caused by the emergence of innovations, which sometimes strongly effect evaluations of existing solutions.

The most challenging thing, however, is to focus sustainable marketing activities on the welfare of consumers in the long term and to determine the limits of interference of external factors in consumer decisions. Related to this process is the occurrence of libertarian paternalism, according to which it is a question of providing the consumer with free choice while narrowing down the available options to the most favourable ones. In effect, the idea is to change consumer behaviour by limiting choice (Thaler, 2018; Thaler & Sunstein, 2017).

Advocates of freedom of choice sometimes criticise libertarian paternalism. Consumers are often irrational and they can take great pleasure in being so. And as long as it does not negatively affect others, they should have the right to be so. The moment external factors (e.g., marketers of goods) externally define what is most beneficial for consumers, they will deprive them of the ability to choose for themselves. Of course, there are situations in which the customer needs such support and asks for it, but this is an entirely different situation to an arbitrary decision that does not consider the consumer's opinion. Precisely programming the fulfilment of consumers' needs according to top-down rules may cause them to feel uncomfortable because of opposition to excessive interference in their lives. People do not like to be manipulated.

On the other hand, however, it must be remembered that the increasing size of the world's population also means an increase in the impact of each person's individual decisions on the lives of others. Making people aware of this fact and minimising negative impacts is something we expect from those shaping modern reality. However, this requires constant control by independent actors to help neutralise attempts to unduly influence consumer behaviour. It is essential because the temptation to use behavioural economics not only to popularise attitudes and behaviours to improve human well-being but also to make commercial gains from such practices is certainly very high (Zuboff, 2019).

In conclusion, the rise in the popularity of sustainable marketing is a fact and it should be regarded as a positive phenomenon. Producers and consumers should be aware of the consequences for the environment and the well-being of all humanity when they make their marketing decisions. Demand for sustainable solutions should be stimulated, and goods and services that are harmful and dangerous to the environment should be stigmatised. When analysing the examples of policies and practices presented in this book, one will appreciate the number of them and how many industries and areas of life are involved. However, deepening the analysis of the practices of the companies implementing them, it can be seen that they are often only single practices not fully integrated in the company's operations. Declarations by companies that listed activities are elements of a circular economy are a bit of a stretch. In many cases, it is clear that the company lacks a holistic pro-environmental view of its activities, while taking a linear approach to production activities. Companies often treat certain pro-environmental practices as screens for the company's actual strategy, which is less sustainable. Many sceptics refer to such behaviour as greenwashing, that is, modifying the information provided to customers about an offering in such a way as to make products appear greener than they are (Gatti et al., 2019). This is because more than two-thirds of consumers are willing to pay more for environmentally friendly products (de Freitas Netto et al., 2020). It has been established (Anwar Abdou et al., 2022) that 'sustainability-marketed products' capture the market faster than ones not so labelled. At the same time, consumers declare (Byrd & Su, 2021) a lack of knowledge about companies' sustainable and pro-environmental activities, which undoubtedly tempts product marketers to use greenwashing.

The evolution of marketing, from a tool used solely to maximise sales of a company's products to an instrument supporting sustainable consumption, is slowly becoming a reality. Consumers feel the need to follow the path of sustainability but they realise that they cannot do it alone. At this point, they are increasingly convinced of the validity of the circular economy concept but at the same time feel that they cannot afford it. This is particularly evident in Polish society, which looks with envy at more developed economies and prioritises achieving the high level of consumption enjoyed in developed countries. Additional environmental standards and other sustainable restrictions are perceived as slowing down the country's economic growth rather than increasing well-being. Without intensive education, this situation will not change very quickly.

Therefore, for sustainable marketing to become a fundamental tool to help realise the aims of a circular economy, education aimed at all market participants is necessary. Today's consumers choose from many more offerings than in the past and find it increasingly difficult to verify information about them. Often, when selecting a source of information, customers are primarily guided by the ease and speed of access to it. In this category, the internet is unrivalled, especially social media, which are generally less reliable than sources of a scientific nature because they contain the random opinions of various people not verified by specialists. It will probably not be possible to eliminate the phenomenon of greenwashing but education on pro-environmental measures can make it possible to sensitise customers to it and thus reduce its effectiveness. Many people and institutions influence today's consumers. When analysing consumer behaviour, creating new pro-environmental education systems and designing sustainable marketing strategies, it is reasonable to include influencers and non-governmental organisations (NGOs) as critical stakeholders in sustainable change. While expecting sustainable decisions to accompany people in every area of their lives, they need to be given the tools to properly assess the impact of these decisions. Financial and organisational support by institutions (state administrations and supranational institutions) for introducing pro-environmental solutions will also be significant. It will help eliminate the social resistance observed in some groups and regions to more sustainable solutions.

An example is using coal to heat individual houses in Poland. Despite being aware of the harmfulness of this solution, householders are often not interested in changing it because they fear an increase in the cost of living. For low-income people, heating constitutes a significant part of their budget. Subsidies for greener energy sources would certainly help allay these fears.

In the traditional organisational structure of enterprises, marketing is generally a tool to support the sales process. However, thanks to the possibility of it being sustainable, it is becoming a management function. The need to implement the assumptions of sustainable marketing and a closed-loop economy necessitates the creation of a marketing information system that will enable the collection of comprehensive data on processes taking place in enterprises and their impact on stakeholders and related environmental issues. Therefore, sustainable marketing should be the responsibility of managers of the entire enterprise, not just the marketing department. The poor state of the environment in Poland makes it particularly important to popularise the assumptions of sustainable marketing in this market. The technological backwardness observed in some areas and the general low level of affluence of society make it possible to assume that it will be difficult to convince most Polish consumers to spend more on sustainably produced products. Therefore, in the case of a country like Poland, the focus should be on popularising the reduction of consumption and food waste, together with such processes as recycling, upcycling, downcycling and reusing. These practices fall within the definition of pro-environmental behaviour and offer a chance to reduce consumer spending. Therefore, it should be easier to convince people to do them.

Shaping the development of sustainable marketing in the operations of enterprises is similar. The first step should be to rationalise spending and consumption in the means of production, and the next step is to employ new more sustainable production technologies. But the most important thing is for entrepreneurs not to stop at single sustainable initiatives but to create holistic strategies to function following the idea of a circular economy.

## References

Anwar Abdou, Y., El-Bassiouny, N., & Becker-Ritterspach, F. (2022). An empirical assessment of the sustainable development goals compass based on consumer sentiment. *Management & Sustainability: An Arab Review*, *1*(1), 66–83. https://doi.org/10.1108/msar-01-2022-0001

Byrd, K., & Su, J. (2021). Investigating consumer behaviour for environmental, sustainable and social apparel. *International Journal of Clothing Science and Technology*, *33*(3), 336–352. https://doi.org/10.1108/IJCST-03-2020-0040

de Freitas Netto, S. V., Sobral, M. F. F., Ribeiro, A. R. B., & Soares, G. R. da L. (2020). Concepts and forms of greenwashing: A systematic review. *Environmental Sciences Europe*, *32*(1). https://doi.org/10.1186/s12302-020-0300-3

Gatti, L., Seele, P., & Rademacher, L. (2019). Grey zone in – Greenwash out. A review of Greenwashing research and implications for the voluntary-mandatory transition of CSR. *International Journal of Corporate Social Responsibility*, *4*(1), 1–15. https://doi.org/10.1186/s40991-019-0044-9

Thaler, R. H. (2018). *Zachowania niepoprawne. Tworzenie ekonomii behawioralnej*. Poznań: Media Rodzina.

Thaler, R. H., & Sunstein, C. R. (2017). *Impuls. Jak podejmować właściwe decyzje dotyczące zdrowia, dobrobytu i szczęścia*. Poznań: Zysk i S-ka Wydawnictwo.

Zuboff, S. (2019). *The Age of Surveillance Capitalism*. London: Profile Books.

# Index


artificial reality 46
attitudes 3, 5, 6, 35, 37–39, 45, 47, 48, 50, 57, 60, 64, 67, 81, 116, 120, 128

biodegradable 18, 33, 93, 121

carbon dioxide emissions, $CO_2$ emissions 11, 75, 82, 95, 100, 112, 118
celebrities 57, 72, 73, 75, 77, 78, 85
celebrity endorsement 72, 78
circular economy concept 8, 11, 13, 76, 128
climate 1–5, 8, 9, 16, 17, 24, 32, 39, 53, 56, 57, 60–62, 64, 71, 74, 75, 79, 81, 83–87, 115, 118, 119, 120, 126
climate change 1, 8, 9, 17, 24, 53, 56, 57, 60–62, 64, 71, 74, 75, 85–87, 118, 119
clothing industry 39, 42, 46
compulsive shopping 41
Corporate Social Responsibility (CSR) 13, 14, 16, 25, 26, 42, 59, 74, 101, 104–106, 109, 110, 112–116, 119, 122–124, 130

deconsumption 37, 38
domocentrism 37

eco-consumption 37, 38
eco-fashion influencers 16; green beauty and skincare influencers 17; outdoor and adventure influencers 16; sustainable parenting influencers 17; upcycling influencers 17; vegan and plant-based influencers 17
eco-friendly 21, 35, 40, 57, 64, 66, 71–73, 75, 76, 81, 85, 116
eco-friendly packaging 35, 91, 93
eco-lifestyle influencers 73, 75, 76
ecological 6, 28, 32–35, 39, 48, 63, 74, 78–81, 84, 90, 93–95, 97, 99, 100, 102, 104, 106–108, 112, 116, 119–122
ecological alternatives 94
ecological awareness 74, 120, 121
ecological business practices 6
ecological materials 93
ecological packaging 100, 119
ecological marketing 32, 33
Ecological Supply Chain Analysis 35
Ecosystem(s) 11, 17, 25, 28, 37, 62, 65, 96, 97
environmental impact(s) 4, 10, 11, 14, 15, 18, 22, 24, 28, 34, 35, 45, 59, 60, 65, 67, 71, 76, 83, 113, 115
environmental protection 2, 48, 63–65, 67, 78–80, 93, 94, 97, 100, 103–105, 108, 111, 112, 116–119, 121
Environmental Social Governance (ESG) 13, 15, 16, 118, 119, 122, 123, 124
environmental marketing 1, 32, 33, 34, 36, 51
environmentally friendly 18, 32, 33, 34, 59, 61, 64, 66, 71, 77, 81–83, 91, 93, 99, 103, 104, 107, 108, 111, 112, 114, 116, 128
environmentally friendly manufacturing 33, 34, 66
ethical marketing 119
European Green Deal 8, 16, 46, 79

Extended Producer Responsibility, EPR 47, 67, 71, 85, 87

fast fashion 39–41, 52, 53, 86
freeganism 37

good practices 16, 26
grassroots organisations 80
green marketing 4, 32–34, 38, 47, 49–52, 120
greenhouse gas emissions 60, 117, 119
greenwashing 5, 6, 19, 43–45, 47–49, 53, 73, 77, 122, 128–130

industrial symbiosis 9, 14, 16, 21, 22, 24, 26, 29
Industry: Chemicals 93, 96
Industry: Clothing 114, 117
Industry: Construction 92, 101, 115, 119
Industry: Construction and real estate 92, 101, 115
Industry: Consulting 104
Industry: E-commerce 118
Industry: Electronics and household appliances 109
Industry: Energy, Recycling 95
Industry: Finance 91, 98, 99, 101, 103, 105, 107, 119
Industry: FMCG 91, 94
Industry: Food 111, 117
Industry: Pharmaceuticals 106, 115
Industry: Raw materials and fuels 97
Industry: Recycling 100
Industry: Services 96, 97, 100, 105, 106, 116
Industry: Telecommunications 102, 111
Industry: Trade 93, 94, 99, 102–104, 106, 108, 110, 118
Industry: Water and sewage 112
Industry: Wood, paper and furniture 98, 112, 113
influencers 53, 57, 72–78, 85, 129
innovative solutions 34, 71, 77, 114, 118, 122

local initiatives 19, 20

marketing orientation 30
media 31, 40, 47, 53, 57, 66, 72, 73, 81, 85, 123, 129, 130
minimising waste 59, 73, 95, 98, 99, 101, 111
Ministry of Climate and Environment 81

natural environment 34, 37, 63, 90, 93, 94, 96, 99, 102, 107, 111, 112, 116, 119, 120
natural resources 4, 8, 10, 13, 17, 32, 36, 37, 62, 64, 66, 104, 105, 114, 118, 121
non-governmental organisations (NGOs) 56, 60, 61–66, 69, 70, 74, 84–87, 105, 129

planned product obsolescence 42, 43, 51, 67, 68, 87
pro-ecological activities 99, 102, 112
pro-ecological attitudes 116
pro-ecological innovations 6, 79
prosumer(s) 12, 38, 43
prosumption 9, 37, 38
protect nature 111
protect the environment 34, 56, 78, 85, 102, 119
protect the planet 99

recycle 38, 40, 43, 67, 68, 83, 115, 118
recycled 18, 20, 41, 46, 59, 91, 103, 108, 117–119
recycled materials 18, 41, 59, 108
recycling 5, 10–13, 17, 19, 21–24, 26–28, 34, 45, 46, 48, 59, 66, 67, 69, 70, 74, 76, 77, 81, 82, 93–95, 99, 100, 102–104, 107–109, 111, 112, 117–122, 129
reduce 13, 18, 34, 38, 40, 43, 45, 46, 59, 61, 65, 67, 69–71, 73, 74, 82, 91–94, 100, 102, 107, 111, 112, 115–117, 129, 130
reduces $CO_2$ 118
repairing 11, 17, 59, 68–70, 101, 108, 109, 113
resistance to sustainable change 58
responsible business 15, 16, 74, 90
responsible consumption 13, 26, 59, 63, 64, 71, 74, 78, 83
responsible consumer choices 63, 74, 101
retro-consumption 37
reusable packaging 100, 118, 121
reusing 23, 59, 96, 106–108, 111, 112, 116, 120, 129

second life 97, 102, 103, 105–107, 110, 111, 114–116
shopaholism 41
slow food 45

slow life 45
Small Medium Enterprises (SMEs) 22, 23, 52
smart shopping 37
social responsibility 13, 25, 31, 42, 54, 59, 61, 62, 66, 74, 86, 109, 110, 119, 130
stakeholders 6, 10, 14, 17, 19, 34, 35, 44, 45, 55–59, 62, 64, 66, 69, 71, 78, 80, 83, 85, 86, 116, 129
stakeholders of sustainable change 56
sustainability 1, 4, 6–10, 13–19, 23–30, 32, 33, 35–39, 42, 43, 45, 47, 48, 51, 57–67, 69–78, 80–89, 93, 110, 114, 117, 120, 122, 123, 126, 128, 130
sustainable approach 31, 35, 94, 95, 110, 113
sustainable change 6, 13, 55–60, 62, 66, 69, 73, 78, 85, 129
sustainable circular 58, 76, 113
sustainable consumer decisions 113
sustainable consumption 6, 22, 28, 37, 45–48, 50–53, 57, 61, 63–65, 67, 71–75, 78, 80, 85, 87, 114, 115, 120, 128
sustainable development 2, 4, 5, 8–10, 13, 17, 23, 27–29, 32, 35–37, 49, 56, 62–65, 78–80, 92, 94, 95, 97, 99, 102, 107, 110–114, 116–122, 130
sustainable influencers 77; climate change activists 74; community and NGO collaborators 74; environmental educators 74; wildlife and nature conservationists 73; zero-waste influencers 73
sustainable lifestyle 76, 96, 101
sustainable marketing 4, 6, 30, 32, 33, 35–39, 45–47, 49, 50, 52, 53, 78, 90–94, 96–109, 111–119, 121, 122, 126–130
sustainable practices 13, 15, 16, 47, 60, 61, 62, 66, 67, 72, 73, 75, 78, 80, 83, 85, 92, 96, 99, 107, 111, 116, 120–122
sustainable social 51, 61, 119
sustainable technologies 6, 66, 70, 92
sustainable consumption 6, 22, 28, 37, 45–48, 50–53, 57, 61, 63–65, 67, 71–75, 78, 80, 85, 87, 114, 115, 120, 128

United Nations 9, 29, 56, 74, 80
upcycling 63, 68, 70, 76, 96, 97, 99, 103, 114, 115, 129

virtual fitting rooms 46

zero-waste 63, 73, 75, 88, 89, 98, 107, 108, 113, 124

Printed in the United States
by Baker & Taylor Publisher Services